BETTER THAN REVIVAL!

Observations on fulfilling the Great Commission

BY KEN CHANT

BETTER THAN REVIVAL!

Observations on fulfilling the Great Commission

By Dr. Ken Chant

Copyright © 2012 Ken Chant

ISBN 978-1-61529-040-6

Vision Publishing
1672 Main St. E 109
Ramona, CA 92065
1-800-9-VISION
www.booksbyvision.com

A NOTE ON GENDER

It is unfortunate that the English language does not contain an adequate generic pronoun (especially in the singular number) that includes without bias both male and female. So *"he, him, his, man, mankind,"* with their plurals, must do the work for both sexes. Accordingly, wherever it is appropriate to do so in the following pages, please include the feminine gender in the masculine, and vice versa.

FOOTNOTES

A work once fully referenced will thereafter be noted either by "ibid" or "op. cit."

CONTENTS

Part One Models Of Revival

Part Two Models Of Revival

Chapter Thirteen

Chapter Fourteen

Chapter Fifteen

ABBREVIATIONS

Abbreviations commonly used for the books of the Bible are

Genesis	Ge	Habakkuk	Hb
Exodus	Ex	Zephaniah	Zp
Leviticus	Le	Haggai	Hg
Numbers	Nu	Zechariah	Zc
Deuteronomy	De	Malachi	Mal
Joshua	Js		
Judges	Jg		
Ruth	Ru	Matthew	Mt
1 Samuel	1 Sa	Mark	Mk
2 Samuel	2 Sa	Luke	Lu
1 Kings	1 Kg	John	Jn
2 Kings	2 Kg	Acts	Ac
1 Chronicles	1 Ch	Romans	Ro
2 Chronicles	2 Ch	1 Corinthians	1 Co
Ezra	Ezr	2 Corinthians	2 Co
Nehemiah	Ne	Galatians	Ga
Esther	Es	Ephesians	Ep
Job	Jb	Philippians	Ph
Psalm	Ps	Colossians	Cl
Proverbs	Pr	1 Thessalonians	1 Th
Ecclesiastes	Ec	2 Thessalonians	2 Th
Song of Songs	Ca *	1 Timothy	1 Ti
Isaiah	Is	2 Timothy	2 Ti
Jeremiah	Je	Titus	Tit
Lamentations	La	Philemon	Phm
Ezekiel	Ez	Hebrews	He
Daniel	Da	James	Ja
Hosea	Ho	1 Peter	1 Pe
Joel	Jl	2 Peter	2 Pe
Amos	Am	1 John	1 Jn
Obadiah	Ob	2 John	2 Jn
Jonah	Jo	3 John	3 Jn
Micah	Mi	Jude	Ju
Nahum	Na	Revelation	Re

Scripture translations are my own unless otherwise noted.

Ca is an abbreviation of *Canticles,* a derivative of the Latin name of the *Song of Solomon*, which is sometimes also called the *Song of Songs*.

Part One

MODELS OF REVIVAL

Chapter One

THE "HESITANT PULPIT" SYNDROME

"Sarcasm," said Thomas Carlyle, "(is) the language of the Devil, for which reason I have, long since, as good as renounced it." However, I am not so noble as the Scottish author, so (as someone else said) although "it is the lowest form of wit", I am going to wax sarcastic.

Think about all those volumes on church growth, and all those magazines and manuals designed for pastors. One wonders how Paul and his colleagues ever managed to build and shepherd successful local churches? What sympathy the unfortunate Timothy and the unhappy Titus must deserve! How could those young men ever have hoped to succeed in ministry without the benefit of attending at least one "church growth" conference each year? Yet somehow they did rather well! Does this mean we have been sold a plastic banana? Perhaps the New Testament is adequate after all as a manual of effective ministry?

So the madness passes, and I am sensible again. No doubt the current array of books, journals, and conferences (or at least some of them) offer modern church leaders much practical benefit. Only a "pompous ignoramus" [1] would cast them aside altogether. Whatever shrewd insight or better method we can employ to enhance the growth and vitality of our churches we should surely use. Yet the best of them may in the end do more harm than good if they cause a feeling that God's method of church planting and building is inadequate.

What is that method?

---

[1]   The expression is Paul's - 1 Timothy 6:4a (REB).

Surely just the word preached in Pentecostal power, and the saints nurtured in godly love -

> *"Christ did not send me to baptise people [2] but to preach the gospel. Even then I do not depend upon eloquence or skill, or else the cross of Christ might be stripped of its power.*

> *"Preaching about the cross seems like nonsense to those who are perishing; but to us who are being saved it is nothing less than the power of God. Is it not written: 'I will destroy the wisdom of the wise, and the learning of the scholars I will throw away'?*

> *"Where then does that leave the wise? What will the clever writer do? How will this world's brilliant debaters fare? God says that if they depend upon their learning then they are fools! Indeed, in his own wisdom, God has made up his mind that the world will never discover him through its philosophy. Instead, he is determined that only by the foolishness of our preaching will those who believe find salvation." [3]*

Suppose our modern insights, marketing strategies, technologies, methods, outreach tools, and all, had been available to Paul, I wonder what use he would have made of them? Would he have ignored them all? Probably not. I think he would have used at least some of those devices of communication and growth; yet I feel sure he would have done so with restraint. It is hard to escape the derisive sense of the passage quoted above - it is more sarcastic than my opening speech! Paul scorned any thought of adding to the gospel secular wisdom and techniques. To fulfil his apostolic

---

2   If Paul were writing this letter today, he might have included here many other aspects of modern ministry, which distract the church from fulfilling its primary function.

3   1 Corinthians 1:17-21.

mandate he was apparently content to depend upon preaching alone, backed up by miracles.

With biting wit he observes how God, by setting up an absurd strategy, mocks all the pretensions of those who reckon themselves wise. Paul was splendidly amused. On one side stands all the cleverness of the world; and on the other, God places - what? A pulpit! There is a ludicrous ambiguity in the Greek text. Was the apostle saying that (according to human wisdom) preaching is a foolish act, or that the gospel is a foolish message, or that we are a bunch of preaching fools? Perhaps he intended to say all three! He certainly leaves little room for any preacher to strut around as if he or she were the very paragon of wisdom! We are all at best fools, preaching foolish sermons, foolishly! But that is the irony of heaven, cutting the world out of the action, so that in the end nothing is left (not even clever preachers and clever sermons) but only the power of the cross.

ADDING TO SCRIPTURE

Our trouble is, we have lost sight of God's method. We have taken Paul's words too seriously. We agree with him too well. From a human perspective it is preposterous to suppose that something as ineffectual as preaching [4] is enough to win the lost and to build the church. So we feel driven to surround the pulpit with a vast apparatus of promotions and property, machinery and methods. We add to the sacred desk the paraphernalia of our techniques, splendid buildings, selling skills, programmes, until the cross can scarcely be seen, and its power is undermined. Few preachers remain confident that so long as they have a Bible in their hands, a tongue in their mouth, and a place to stand, they have all they truly need to fulfil the demands of the evangel.

---

4   Let us be honest enough to admit that few of the occupiers of our pulpits across the centuries have ever deserved to be called orators. As public speakers, qualified speech-makers, crowd-movers, powerful exhorters, most preachers would never find secular employment!

Some years ago I discovered in a large local church no less than eight pastors who were sitting in the pews. They were neither on the staff of the church nor ministering, but were simply members of the congregation. The sight of them worshipping patiently Sunday after Sunday provoked me to make some enquiries. I learned that they were all expecting to resume their ministry eventually, but felt that they had to wait for a church to "call" them. Having sent out resumés to many places, they now sat inactive, hoping for the mail to bring them a suitable invitation (especially one offering an excellent salary).

I was astonished. I tackled each of them with the same challenge: Why do you keep on warming these pews, waiting for someone to hand you a church on a platter? Why don't you get out into the teeming fields and reap a harvest of your own? They looked at me with dismay. Not one of them had enough confidence in his preaching to believe that he needed only a pulpit to build a church. Eventually they were driven one by one back into secular employment, while they continued to send out hopeful applications to church boards around the country.

"But," someone may protest, "perhaps they were not good speakers?" Paul scorned oratory. Another cries, "I am not handsome, and my voice is squeaky." Paul had a mean physical appearance, [5] and probably unimpressive vocal gifts. Someone else says, "I lack money and equipment." What did Paul have other than the message of the cross preached in the power of the Holy Spirit? Still another complains, "But I have a family to care for, I need the income, I can't afford to pioneer a church." Then work with your hands, as Paul did, while he kept on preaching until each church he pioneered was large enough to meet his financial needs.

---

5   2 Co 10:1,10, "Face to face, his presence is insignificant, his appearance is unremarkable, and as a preacher he is beneath contempt!"

HAVING SOMETHING TO SAY

The only important question is this: has God called you to preach? If so, why do you doubt that you will succeed in doing it as well as he requires? I once read a volume of poems by the Canadian writer Robert Service, which he composed while he was living in the Bohemian quarter of Paris, on the eve of the First World War. He tells how in May 1914 he met another poet with the odd name of Saxon Dane, who said:

> *"The trouble with poetry is that it is too exalted. It has a phraseology of its own; it selects themes that are outside of ordinary experience. As a medium of expression it fails to reach the great mass of the people."*

Then he added -

> *"To hell with the great mass of the people! What have they got to do with it? Write to please yourself, as if not a single reader existed. The moment a man begins to be conscious of an audience he is artistically damned. You're not a Poet I hope?"*

I meekly assured him I was a mere maker of verse.

> *"Well,"* said he, *"better good verse than middling poetry . . . Let each one who has something to say, say it in the best way he can, (and then be content to) abide the result."* [6]

What is true of poets is true of preachers. If you have something to say, then say it as well as you can, and leave the rest in God's hands. The best preachers, too, do not preach for the people. They follow the rule: preach "to please God" - "as if not a single hearer

---

6   Ballads Of A Bohemian, Book One, "Spring"; T. Fisher Unwin, London, 1921; pg. 63-64.

existed." You may not be "artistically damned" if you become too conscious of your audience, but you will certainly inhibit your effectiveness in serving the Lord.

The gifted Dutch artist Rembrandt (1606-69), when he was just twenty-one years old, encountered a couple of older and well-established artists in a café in Leyden. They enquired when he would follow the example of other aspiring artists, and travel to Italy to continue his studies. Rembrandt announced that he had no interest in going to Italy. The Italian artists, said he, could teach him nothing. Indeed, since he was a Dutchman, not an Italian, he intended to develop a Dutch style. The older men remonstrated with him. What hope could there be that lowly Holland would produce a Raphael or a Da Vinci? The young Rembrandt retorted that Holland would produce something better: his own work!

If you are called by God to the ministry that is the kind of confidence you too should have. Along with the divine call came sufficient ability for you to fulfil it. Of course you should apply yourself diligently to your task, honing your skills as a preacher to the finest quality you can achieve; and of course you should use whatever tools and resources are available to you. You must work hard every way you can to build success in ministry. But in the end, you need nothing more than the call of God. Whether or not you possess the kind of skills the world deems essential for a public speaker, if you are chosen by God, and are obedient to God, you can successfully do the work of God.

The insight of a pirate may help us here -

> *"It was a saying of Captain Blood's that the worth of a man manifests itself not so much in the ability to plan great undertakings as in the vision which perceives opportunity and the address which knows how to seize it."* [7]

---

7   Rafael Sabatini, The Chronicles of Captain Blood (1931), Chapter Two, "The Treasure Ship".

The church of Jesus Christ has no richer treasure, no more powerful agency, no other essential apparatus, than a pulpit and the men and women who stand behind it. Those preachers do not have to be splendidly endowed with natural abilities (1 Co 1:20,26-28; 3:18-19); they need only be anointed by the Father for their glorious task - and in the local church there is no higher, nor more necessary task (Ac 6:2,4). Let no one in the church ever doubt it: "by the foolishness of preaching those who believe will find salvation."

Chapter Two

THE "GIFTED MINISTRY"

SYNDROME

Local churches have allowed the "big names" to demote them to inferior status. The people often feel they have to go to some other place or ministry to obtain a miracle from God, that there is little power in their home church. The great ministries themselves frequently encourage that very attitude. Now there is certainly a vital role for "name" ministries, especially on the national stage, and for preaching to the unsaved. Let us give them all honour; nonetheless, we should avoid setting up "heroes". Rather, we should assess people more wisely, by character - not by outward appearance alone, nor by mere statistical success.

A MUSLIM FABLE

A renowned mullah once chose to attend a glittering banquet disguised as a poor beggar. The rich and noble guests jostled and abused him, the servants struck him and pushed him away from the tables, no wines or delicacies were offered to him. After a while, he left the banquet, returned home, and dressed again, this time in the finest robes, resplendent with many sparkling jewels. On his head he placed an elegantly caparisoned turban, glowing rubies adorned his fingers, and a dazzling gold-threaded sash embellished his costly gown. When he returned to the palace and walked haughtily into the banqueting hall, several ushers rushed to escort him, bowing low. The assembled lords and ladies swarmed around, greeting and honouring him. Then servants presented him with silver trays, laden with sweet things. At once he opened wide his capacious sleeve, and commanded them to pour the dainties and wines into its gaping mouth. When they expressed astonishment he retorted that surely they should feed his garment, and not him, since plainly they honoured the cloth more than the man. Without his robe, they had treated him like offal; with it, they now fell at his feet. How could they deny that it was not him but his robe they revered, which they should therefore surely feed?

Likewise, 1000 years ago, among Buddhists in Japan, the same "hero" syndrome was apparent (there is indeed "nothing new under the sun"!) -

> *"Who pays any attention to a Palace Chaplain when he walks by? Though he may recite the scriptures in a most impressive manner, and may even be quite good-looking, women despise a low-ranking priest, which is very sad for him. Yet, when this same man becomes a Bishop or Archbishop, people are overwhelmed with awe and respect, and everyone is convinced that the Buddha himself has appeared among them!"* [8]

But we have scant cause to feel superior to those follies. Have I not observed in the church men being honoured simply because of their achievements, with little regard for their character? All too often we revere the "garment" more than the man. Let someone come to us garbed with great success and how we bow and scrape! But let the same person arrive unrecognised and we will scarcely show him courtesy. We stand under James' indictment -

> *"My brothers and sisters, how can you claim to believe in our glorious Lord Jesus Christ yet go on showing favour to some and not others? Suppose a man comes among you wearing gold rings and fine*

---

8   The Pillow Book of Sei Shonagon; tr. by Ivan Morris; Penguin Classics, 1967; pg. 193. Sei Shonagon was a lady-in-waiting to the empress in the royal court of Japan.

clothes, [9] *and at the same time a poor man in dirty clothes* [10] *also arrives. Do you highly honour the well-dressed man, saying, 'Please take the best seat,' while you tell the poor man, 'Stand over there,' or, 'Sit here on the floor'? If so, then you are guilty of making false distinctions between people; you have allowed your choices to be governed by evil motives. You would do better, dear friends, to mark this: it is God himself who has chosen those who are poor in this world to be rich in faith and to inherit the kingdom that he has promised to all who love him. Why then do you dishonour the poor?"* [11]

In any case, who is poor and who is rich? Those who today have nothing may tomorrow have everything; and those who are acclaimed today may tomorrow be forgotten. Yet neither estate really matters. We should treat both conditions with indifference. "Rich" or "poor" in human reckoning, our joy in the Lord should remain unchanged -

"Let every poor Christian rejoice when God raises him up, and let every rich Christian rejoice when God brings him down!" [12]

Since none of us know in what situation any of us will be found tomorrow, it is senseless either to adulate the successful or to disdain the unsuccessful. The fortunes of both may tomorrow be reversed. That great man you so admire today, you may tomorrow blush to speak his name. That humble man you spurned today, you may tomorrow yearn to call your friend. Is there someone who has done great things for the kingdom of God? Such people, for the

---

9   Read here, "a huge congregation, a successful ministry, a multi-million dollar facility"!

10 Read here, "a seemingly insignificant pastor of a small church".

11 James 2:1-6.

12 James 1:9-10.

sake of their work, deserve our admiration and respect, perhaps even our praise. But adulation belongs to no one except Christ. So away with the foolish distinctions this world makes! Let us rather bestow equal honour upon all whose lives reflect the beauty of Christ.

BELITTLING YOURSELF

One of the unhappiest consequences of the "gifted ministry" syndrome is this: pastors demolish their effectiveness by constantly promoting other more "successful" ministries. They praise some great pastor from their pulpits; they talk enviously about the huge church the other man or woman leads; they plead with their people to raise enough money to allow them to fly interstate or overseas to visit the great leader's church. And all the time they are unconsciously saying to their people: "this church of ours is little, poor, and inadequate, and I am frustrated, and discontented." Not surprisingly, the people accept their pastor's feelings as true, and decide to go looking for a better church themselves!

A pastor who does not reckon his church is the greatest in the world, whatever size it may be, hardly deserves to be its shepherd. Are you a pastor? How do you measure your congregation? By its numerical size? Then you will never be satisfied, no matter how big it grows. Your restless vexation will inescapably communicate itself to your people, who will become as unhappy as you are. Rather, you should measure your church by its quality of fellowship and love, and reckon your congregation the most wonderful group of people on earth! You will not only be much happier yourself, but your church will probably grow bigger as well!

THE BODY OF CHRIST

The local church should be the major place of healing and of growth toward maturity for every Christian. Wise pastors will never encourage their people to look outside the local church for anything that lies in the promise and purpose of God. If you are a pastor then you should have enough confidence in yourself and in your ministry, and in the leadership team that works with you, to urge the people always to turn first to their own church. James, for example, had no doubt that the "elders of the (local) church" possessed all the grace and power necessary to bring healing to the sick, providing both they and the sick person knew how to offer a "prayer of faith". Those elders, said he, may stand unashamed alongside Elijah when the time comes to unleash spiritual power! (5:13-17).

Now I do not mean that pastors should never make use of outside ministry, nor ever go to conferences or conventions, nor ever take their people to a bigger church. That would be silly. We can all learn from others, and be enriched by the diverse ministries Christ has set in his world-wide church. But I do mean that you should never allow yourself to lapse into some feeling of inferiority or inadequacy merely because your congregation may not be large in numbers. Focus rather on two things:

> ➢ make your congregation huge in spirit, glorious in love, splendid in grace, wealthy in fellowship, ever-advancing in Christ, and you will have no need to envy any other pastor anywhere in the world!

> ➢ function as the true body of Christ in your community; that is, become in your neighbourhood all that Jesus himself would be if he were there in person.

Actually, Jesus is there in person, for each local church is (or should be) the physical presence of Christ in its community. Whatever the people who met Jesus in Palestine long ago could gain from his hand, the people in your district should be able to find in your church. You are Jesus in that area; you are his hands, his heart, his faith, his power. If that is true, what higher gift could you truly want from God? Was Jesus any less because he had only twelve disciples, and one of them a traitor? Are you better than he? Is it not enough that his life and love flow into and out of the local church, which is his body in that place? What can mere bigness add to that inestimable privilege?

Chapter Three

THE "UNEXPECTED REVIVAL" SYNDROME

There are two sources of growth in the kingdom of God -

DIVINE VISITATION

What wonderful days they are, when the Lord pours out his Spirit upon the land, when the fields bend before the sickle of God, and a magnificent harvest of souls is reaped! We read about such times in history, or hear about them happening in some part of the world today, and how we envy those people their good fortune, yearning that we ourselves might experience the same kind of visitation!

For such times we should certainly pray (see Is 64:1-2; Ps 80:3,7,19; etc.), and we should always be ready to respond, for who knows when the wind of the Spirit might suddenly sweep across the land?

Nonetheless, it is true to say that the major New Testament focus is not upon such uncertain and unpredictable heavenly visitations, but rather upon

HUMAN VOLITION

Let us note at once that "visitation" is not a New Testament concept - at least, not after the day of Pentecost. Rather, those first Spirit-filled Christians prayed for boldness to preach the word, expecting that the Lord would confirm their proclamation with signs, wonders, and miracles (Mk 16:20; Ac 4:24-31).

Contrary to that brave spirit, we have adopted a defeatist attitude that cause us to feel helpless to fulfil the evangel unless God gives us a mighty "revival". [13] But that dependency upon divine action has induced a fatalistic passivity that is a pestilence upon the whole church. We have reversed the pattern of the Great Commission, which tells us to go out in the power of the Spirit and to do the work of God. Instead, we want God to do it for us, by sending us a revival, and for revival we endlessly plead.

Yet the command is not "stay at home and pray", but "go out, plant churches, and make disciples" (cp. Ac 11:19-21).

GOD'S STRATEGY

I will come back to the proper use of prayer in the next "Syndrome", but here let me reply to a question I was asked to address at a gathering of pastors: "What is God's strategy today for world evangelisation?"

My answer was immediate and simple: God does not have, and never has had, any such strategy!

Does that surprise you? Then consider this -

> *"When God first thought kindly about the Gentiles,*
> *his plan was to take out from among them a people*
> *who would carry his name"* (Ac 15:14).

That plan has not changed. It conforms to the "remnant" theme that is constant in scripture. At no time has it been the Father's fixed intention to win the whole world to the Christian faith, for if it were, we would have to say that God has been utterly thwarted by human rebellion. But that is impossible. God is in heaven, and does whatever he pleases, both in heaven and on earth! (Ps 115:3; 135:6). If he intended to save all, then all would be saved. But he did not. He intended only to "call out from among the nations a people who would carry his name". That is what he has done, and will continue to do.

---

13   Part Two, below, takes up the theme of "revival" in greater detail.

Notice also Satan's claim (which Jesus did not dispute) that "all the kingdoms of this world and their glory" belong to him and are his to give to anyone he chooses (Lu 4:6). One day, of course, Christ will be given absolute sovereignty over all the earth; but for now only one thing fully belongs to him, and that is his church, purchased with his own blood. One day he will have glory in the nations; but for now, he has glory only in his church (Ep 3:21). [14] So we cannot claim any people, nor even any city, for Christ. Human society, in its fallen state, does not belong to him but to Satan - "the whole world lies under the control of the Evil One" (1 Jn 5:19). Having sold themselves to the devil, the nations of this world are under his command, and must remain so until Christ, on that great coming day, imposes his own irresistible authority. In the meantime, he is "waiting" for the hour when his enemies will be made to lie prostrate before him -

> *"After Christ once and for all had offered the single sacrifice for sin, he sat down at the right hand of God, and there he is now waiting until God compels his enemies to become a footstool under his feet"* (He 10:12-13).

We too, with Christ, look forward to the day when we shall "rule the nations with a rod of iron" (Re 2:26-27); but that day is not yet. We shall possess the earth then; we cannot possess it now. It will then be ours by right; but for now Satan has that right, and we cannot deny it to him.

But we can do what we are told to do: that is, fulfil the evangel, go out, plant churches, make disciples, and get as many people as we can thoroughly out of hell and thoroughly into heaven.

---

[14] I do not mean that Christ lacks power to seize whatever he desires on earth, including any and every nation. He cannot do that, however. Not because he lacks the strength, but because the laws of heaven cannot be violated. The devil's power over the nations belongs to him legally, by divine fiat (cp. Re 13:7), and the time has not yet come for the Lord God to re-assert his sovereignty.

How much growth can we rightly expect? Never forget that Christ has assured his church of success in general (Mt 16:18), but not in particular (Lu 10:10-11). Any single church may fall, or be destroyed by the enemy's savagery; any single missionary enterprise may fail. But collectively, the church of Jesus Christ is invincible, its mandate irresistible, and the Lord has guaranteed that until the very end of the age there will remain a harvest waiting to be reaped!

FEW ARE SAVED

You might also think about this. There was an occasion when the disciples came to Jesus and asked him how many people will enter the kingdom (Lu 13:22). His answer was unequivocal: only a few will be saved (vs. 23; Mt 7:13-14). Now across the entire span of redemption history that "few" will eventually equal "a great multitude, more than anyone can count, from every nation, tribe, people, and language" (Re 7:9); but at any one time or in any one place most people have always chosen, and will continue to choose, the wide road that leads to destruction and not the narrow path that leads to life. In any particular community, salvation comes to the "few" not to the "many". Indeed, at the end of the age, Christ wondered if he would find any faith on the earth! (Lu 18:8)

Look at it this way: suppose Jesus were here now, visiting Sydney, and someone were to walk up to him and ask the same question he was asked in the gospel: "Lord, will only a few people be saved?" What would he say? That Sydney will soon be so shaken by a visitation of God that it will become a bastion of righteousness in the world? That the greater part of its four million people will be saved. That the hour of visitation could be hastened if only more people would pray for revival? Or would his reply be the same today as it was then? "The way into the kingdom is narrow, and only those who earnestly strive [15] for it will ever find it."

Does this mean we should neither pray for nor expect a visitation of God upon our city or land? Of course not. But it should temper our expectations to a more realistic level and provoke us not to keep on supinely waiting for some possibly mythical "revival". Rather, let the church get busy with the work of the kingdom! Perhaps we cannot win everyone to Christ, or even the majority, or even many - but we can certainly win some, and so stay partners with God in "calling out from the nation a people for his name"!

---

[15] The Greek word is (*agonidzomai*), from which comes our word "agonise". It has something of the same meaning in Greek, although it was more particularly linked with athletic contests, where it had the idea of competing fiercely for the prize, exerting every possible effort, contending and fighting with all one's strength, undeterred by pain or exhaustion

Chapter Four

THE "PRAYER FOR REVIVAL" SYNDROME

At another gathering of Christian leaders I was asked how much time we should devote to "intercessory prayer for national revival"? It is a question that worries many devout people, who are deeply troubled by the thought that perhaps they are not praying as fervently or as frequently as they should, and therefore "revival" is hindered. My questioner wondered how much prayer was necessary: an hour a day, an hour a week - or more - or less?

Underlying such questions is an assumption that in fact revival can be, and must be, promoted by prayer. Only let enough Christians pray with enough fervour for long enough, and revival must surely follow. But how many, how much, how long? That is the great unknown.

I would rather ask: what reliance can we place on this assumption that revival is an inevitable consequence of the right kind of prayer? In my opinion, the surmise is false. There is no biblical evidence that prayer can produce massive church growth independently of other external factors.

Before you start throwing rocks, notice the underlined clause, which I will return to in a moment. In the meantime, someone is probably saying: "What about the first few chapters of Acts. Didn't the early church pray successfully for a great move of God?" (Ac 4:24-31; 5:12-16). Note two things -

UNREPEATABLE EVENTS

Those astonishing events in old Jerusalem were never repeated, and the story in Acts actually confirms my claim: that is, those first prayer meetings were not held in a social or historical vacuum.

They occurred against the staggering background of the three years of Jesus' ministry, the events of his Passion, the Pentecostal event, the healing of the crippled man (Ac 3:1 ff.) - and all this in a city that was groaning under foreign oppression. In other words, in old Jerusalem there was a peculiar set of unrepeatable circumstances that made the city ripe for a great harvest of souls.

Within that environment, the cry of the disciples - "O Lord, stretch out your hand to heal, and to perform signs and wonders through the name of your holy servant Jesus" - irresistibly attracted a powerful answer from heaven. [16] But since then, how many others have raised a similar plea to God, yet without anything like the same response? Why does heaven remain silent? Simply because the kind of spiritual environment that existed in ancient Jerusalem during those first years has seldom, if ever, been repeated. When the external factors are appropriate, then prayer can unlock an incredible surge of growth in the church; but lacking those factors, prayer alone can achieve little. [17]

Not only was there no repetition of those first Jerusalem years in the later history of the church, there is also a lack of any instruction to pray for such a repetition. Search where you will, you will find no command in the New Testament to "pray for revival", or for "an outpouring of the Spirit", or for "a move of God", or to "claim a city (or a nation) for Christ", or anything of the sort. But you will find plenty of exhortations to get out into the harvest field (whether the crop is sparse or munificent), and to get on with the job of

---

16   Note also, that they prayed only once. The outpoured Spirit did not result from repeated, continuous, or prolonged prayer, but from just one single, bold, believing request. There is no example here of the kind of endless, repeated intercessions for "revival" that are often promulgated as a burden earnest Christians must assume. Remember also that the majority of the citizens and their leaders (both political and religious) continued to reject the gospel. Despite the "revival", the Christians remained a minority group.

17   The second part of this study, "Models of Revival", will take up this theme in more detail.

planting churches (whether small or large), and of making disciples, until Jesus comes.

NATIONAL REVIVAL

Someone else may now start waving at me the promise in 2 Chronicles 7:14. Is there not here a command to start praying and keep on praying until God opens the heavens and pours out his Spirit over the entire land?

That text and others like it are applicable to us Christians only in a limited sense. They were spoken to Israel, which was a nation in covenant relationship with God. There is no such covenant between God and Australia. This nation cannot be described as "his people". There is no promise in scripture that "revival" may be had by Australia, if only the church would humble itself and pray. Old Testament promises to Israel of national revival are no longer valid in a territorial sense; they cannot be applied to the nation, but must speak rather to the church. That is, the church now comprises "his people", and to us the promise comes of spiritual health and wellbeing in response to trustful prayer.

Admittedly, a vigorous and flourishing church, acting as "the salt and yeast" of the earth (Mt 5:13; 13:33), can draw a nation toward righteousness, and therefore attract the favour of God (Pr 14:34; Ps 144:15) - but that is simply the natural benefit reaped by a nation that has allowed the church to expand and permeate it from border to border, and has permitted the preaching of the gospel to shape its policies toward godliness (Pr 20:28; 25:4-5).

Against that background we discover that the New Testament teaching on prayer is focussed on two things -

(1) They prayed for individual growth into holiness and maturity rather than enlargement of a congregation. The apostles showed little interest in how to achieve numerical growth in a local church; but they never stopped emphasising the need for every believer to strive for holiness. Whether the Christians were few or many, the

apostles wanted every one of them to display the character and strength of the risen Christ in all their words and actions. See, for example, Ephesians 1:15-19 and Colossians 1:9-12. Here is an apostle praying constantly for a church. What does he ask for?

> ➢ Revival?

> ➢ Many decisions for Christ?

> ➢ Material or financial supply?

> ➢ Success in their ministry?

No! You will not find in his petition even one of the items that endlessly occupy most congregational prayers today. He wanted only one thing, that "they might conduct themselves in a way that is pleasing to the Lord, being fruitful in every good work, and growing in the knowledge of God." For the rest, he was content to leave their destiny in the hands of God. He knew well enough that some churches for their faithfulness will reap abundant blessing, while others will suffer persecution, robbery, and death (cp. He 11:32-38).

So then, in some towns, in some countries, the church finds a welcome, and great is its prosperity and growth; in others it meets with hatred and rejection, and must accept cheerfully the plundering of all its goods and the loss of all that it prizes (10:32-36). For that reason, the apostles added one other focus to their teaching on prayer -

(2) They prayed for a safe environment for effective ministry - see 1 Timothy 2:1-4. Now that passage is particularly interesting, for it answers the question about how we should pray for the nation. Does Paul instruct Timothy to pray for revival to surge across the land, or to claim the nation for Christ? No. He tells him rather to ask God to bend the government toward creating a peaceful and open community. Then the church would be able to work quietly and freely at the task of spreading the gospel. Paul highly commends such prayers, saying that they are "proper and pleasing

in the sight of God". Why? Because "God desires that everyone should be saved and come to know the truth."

Think about that!

Here is Paul expressing the very goal that underlies our craving for "revival": mass conversions to Christ. But Paul says that we can reach that goal, not by fervent cries for a visitation of God, but rather by quietly keeping busy with the work of the kingdom, spreading the gospel to every part of the land. And, says Paul, if the rulers hinder that task, then pray for them. Not for God to by-pass them or crush them by a mighty outpouring of the Spirit, but that he will change the political and social milieu, so that the church can obediently fulfil its missionary mandate. [18]

FARM LABOURERS

Several of the analogies Jesus used show that in the kingdom of God a fruitful harvest depends primarily upon the same things that govern prosperity on the farm. They are -

HARD WORK

The Father of mankind himself has willed
The path of husbandry should not be smooth;
He first disturbed the fields with human skill,
Sharpening the wits of mortal men with care,
Unwilling that his realm should sleep in sloth . . .
He put foul poison in the serpent's fang,
And ordered wolves to plunder, seas to rage . . .
So that experience by taking thought
Might gradually hammer out the arts,

---

18 See my book Mountain Movers (Chapter Seven), for more comment on this matter, and on prayer in general.

And in the furrows seek the blade of corn. [19]

I have observed pastors blaming Satan for their woes when they would have been wiser to meditate on Proverbs 6:9-11; 24:30-34, and then arouse themselves from laziness. They are like that indolent fellow who cried, "There is a lion roaming abroad; there is a lion prowling loose; I will surely be killed if I go outside!" (Pr 22:13; 26:13) They blame a lion for their poverty when the real problem is lethargy. [20] In the metaphors of the "footpad", the "armed bandit", and the "lion", we may well see an image of Satan. But the lesson remains: lack of diligence alone opened the way for the robber to come and despoil the landowner or the householder.

Out on the farm there is an unspoken presumption: the right kind of hard work will bring prosperity. No farmer who is ruled by sloth can hope for success. The same is ordinarily true for those who are labouring to build a local church. However, just as farmers have different levels of skill, so that while one can manage at best a small property another may run a huge conglomerate, so are pastors different from each other. Also, no matter how well a farm is run, it may suffer drought, or famine, or war, or pestilence, and all the farmer's labour may be lost.

Similar misfortunes can overwhelm a local church. The wise farmer is ready both to flourish and to fail, and still to give praise to the Lord -

> *"Though the fig tree fails to blossom, and there is no fruit on the vines; though the olive trees produce nothing, and every harvest fails; though the animals die in the fields and all the stalls stand empty; yet I will keep on rejoicing in the Lord, I will make merry*

---

19   Publius Vergilius Maro (Virgil) (70-19 B.C.), The Georgics - Book One; tr. K. R. Mackenzie; The Folio Society, London, 1969; pg. 17.

20   Here are some more references to the poverty the slothful deserve, and exhortations to diligence: Pr 10:5; 13:4; 15:19; 18:9; 19:15; 20:4,13; 21:25; 22:13; 26:16; Ec 10:18; Mt 25:26-30; Ro 12:11; 2 Th 3:11-13; He 6:12.

with the God of my salvation, for the Lord God himself is all my strength!" (Ha 3:17-19).

"When everything is going well for you, be glad; and if everything goes wrong, consider this: poverty and prosperity both come from God, and you cannot tell which one it will be" (Ec 7:14).

So there is no final guarantee of success on any particular patch of land. Nonetheless, usually if you work hard you can expect to gain the reward of your labour. Beware, however, of confusing true work with merely packing each day with frenetic activity:

"Yet, after all, the truly efficient labourer will not crowd his day with work, but will saunter to his task, surrounded by a wide halo of ease and leisure, and then do what he loves best. He is anxious only about the fruitful kernels of time. Though the hen should sit all day, she could lay only one egg, and, besides, would not have picked up the materials for another. Let a man take time enough for the most trivial deed, though it be but the paring of his nails. The buds swell imperceptibly, without hurry or confusion, as if the short spring days were all eternity.
Then spend an age in whetting thy desire,
Thou need'st not hasten if thou dost stand fast." [21]

Remember too that all work is made worthless unless it springs from a motive of love (1 Co 13:1-3) -

"Work is love made visible. . . .
(But) if you bake bread with indifference, you bake
a bitter bread
that feeds but half man's hunger.

---

21   Henry David Thoreau (1817-62), American essayist and poet, A Week on the Concord and Merrimack Rivers; Heritage Press, Norwalk CT; 1975; pg. 86, 87. See also the further note below.

And if you grudge the crushing of the grapes,
your grudge distils a poison in the wine.
And if you sing though as angels, and love not the
singing,
you muffle man's ears to the voices of the day
and the voices of the night. [22]

Another illustration of the pragmatic need for hard work stands in the scripture itself, and it consists of the entire Book of Esther. God is not once mentioned in Esther. [23] Does that silence have any significance?

"The Deity is not seen or even heard on (Esther's)
stage, (yet) God is standing in the wings, following
the drama and arranging the props for a successful
resolution of the play...

---

[22]   Kahlil Gibran, The Prophet; Alfred A. Knopf, New York, 1968; pg. 28.

[23]   That is, in the Hebrew text. In the Greek version, the words "Lord" or "God" occur more than 50times. Those differences are themselves indicative of the two kinds of piety: on the one hand, the pragmatic view of the Hebrew author; and on the other, the pious view of his Greek counterpart. The first writer understood that the Lord ordinarily works "behind the scenes", unseen, unheard, unfelt, allowing people freedom of action, yet still ensuring that nothing of his purpose should fail. The second writer wanted God to be more visible, actively involved in human affairs, firmly controlling every event, overtly and plainly at work governing the fortunes of his people. The same conflicting pieties are evident in the church today - although ironically, the very people who are most adamant in defending the full historicity and accuracy of the canonical Esther are the same ones who usually embrace the kind of piety preferred by the Greek version (which they reject as non-canonical)!

The Greek version, by the way, is designated "deutero-canonical" by the Roman Catholic and Orthodox churches, and is always included in their editions of the Bible. (The books known as the "Apocrypha" by Protestants are called "deutero-canonical" by Catholics and Orthodox, in distinction from the other books in the Bible, which they call "proto-canonical".)

The author is saying that, as in the case of Mordecai and Esther, Providence can be relied upon to reverse the ill-fortunes that beset individuals or the nation - provided that such leaders and their followers actively do their part, acting wisely and courageously." [24]

The exclusion at the end of that passage is important: God seldom acts except through the willing co-operation and active participation of his servants. So the story of Esther unfolds around the shrewd common-sense of Mordecai, the bravery of Queen Esther, her strategy of making herself as lovely as possible when she approached Xerxes, her plan to attract his favour by inviting him to two banquets, and the clever way in which she revealed Haman's treachery. Haman was ruined, and deliverance came to the Jews. In the background, unseen, unheard, the hand of the Lord is also at work, enabling Mordecai to render the king some useful service, setting the scene for Haman's embarrassment, causing Xerxes to receive Esther favourably and to attend her banquet, helping the Jews to defend themselves against their foes, and the like. Perhaps also, early in the story, we may assume that God helped that admirable lady, Queen Vashti, who so bravely defied the king's command.

The lesson we must learn from all these things is that hard work, courage, shrewd planning, and undaunted persistence are vital keys to success in the harvest field. God seldom does for people what they can do for themselves.

INNATE SKILL

I will have more to say about this in a later "Syndrome"; but here let us note at least these two things: no one can achieve anything higher than his or her skill allows; only the absurd struggle to be what they are not -

"But try," you urge, "the trying shall suffice:

---

24   From the "Introduction to Esther", in The New Oxford Annotated Bible; Oxford University Press, New York, 1991; pg. 612. Emphasis mine.

The aim, if reached or not, makes great the life.
Try to be Shakespeare, leave the rest to fate!"
Spare my self-knowledge - there's no fooling me!
If I prefer remaining my poor self,
I say so not in self-dispraise but praise.
If I'm a Shakespeare, let the well alone -
Why should I try to be what now I am?
If I'm no Shakespeare, as too probable, -
His power and consciousness and self-delight
And all we want in common, shall I find -
Trying for ever? [25]

How many hours of practice does it take to turn a ham-fisted, tone-deaf, musically inept person into a concert pianist? Will the purchase of acres of canvas and gallons of paint transform a colour-blind, finger-clumsy person into a renowned artist? Were I to give you a mallet and chisel and a perfect block of marble, could you then carve a replica of even the least of Michelangelo's sculptures? Like the worthy bishop in Browning's poem, not even if we tried for ever could any of us conjure up "Shakespeare's power and consciousness", nor find a way to supply all that "we want in common" with the great dramatist.

In any case, if you happen to be another Shakespeare, why should you try to be what you already are? And if not, what purpose is there in trying? Better for all of us if we simply prefer to remain who we are, and to do what we can do. And, with the bishop, we can say that, "not in self-dispraise but praise" - for there is no shame in fulfilling the person God made you to be. Why should you question his providence? Shall a pot complain to its maker about the way it has been shaped? (Ro 9:20-21). Some farmers are better than others; they have innate abilities that their neighbours lack. Those with skills should not deny them; those without,

25 From Bishop Blougram's Apology, by Robert Browning (1812-89). The bishop is debating with an unbeliever, who urges upon him the virtue of striving for the highest levels of achievement; to which the cleric replies in the above words.

should not envy them. Rather, such skills as we each have, let us employ them to the full for the Father's glory. And be content to recognise the inescapable limits placed upon us, both by the gifts we possess and those we lack.

PROPER ENVIRONMENT

Observation of life on a farm confirms what I have said above: prayer for "revival" cannot be effective unless the environment is congenial to a spiritual awakening and a great harvest. Every farmer knows that the prosperity of his farm depends upon fertile soil, good rains, stable seasons, freedom to work, and the like. Otherwise, despite an avalanche of prayer, his crop must inevitably fail, and his affluence will collapse. Many a godly, hard-toiling farmer, attacked by flood, fire, earthquake, famine, drought, or some other disaster, has watched helplessly while nature's violence ravaged his life's work beyond repair.

Here is a different illustration of the same principle. Much contemporary literature from the time of the Crusades has survived, from both sides in the wars. The reports reveal a striking fact: Christians and Muslims were equally fervent in their claims of divine support. Both armies praised God when they won a battle and blamed their own sins when they lost. The reader soon realises that in most cases victory or defeat had much more to do with military than spiritual factors. Now one side prevails, then the other, until, after centuries of bitter conflict, the Muslims triumphed and the Christians, with terrible slaughter, were driven out of the Holy Land. Here is one report, from the Muslim side, as told by an Egyptian writer of the time, Badr al-Din al-Aini -

> *"With God's help, the Mamluks landed in Cyprus on Thursday 4 July 1426, and immediately set up camp ... The Mamluks set their ladders against the castle walls, but these did not reach high enough. One of them, having divested himself of his armour, succeeded in climbing on to the top of the*

battlements. God gave him strength for the sake of the Prophet Mohammed - may he be praised . . . He was soon followed by the others; once inside, they killed the Franks who had gone into hiding and, having captured the castle, they raised the sultan's banner, sang God's praises and blessed the Prophet." [26]

So too in the life of the church. Natural factors cannot be ignored when calculating the prospects of substantial growth. No matter how hard a farmer works, he will never grow a crop on a slab of rock. But then, even if his fields are wondrously fertile, he will still not prosper unless he does work hard. As Paul said (in a different context, but the rule is universal): "the spiritual does not come first, but the physical, and then the spiritual" (1 Co 15:46). Get the natural environment right, and a good harvest will usually follow, especially if the farmer threads prayer through every aspect of his life and labour.

GODLINESS

According to the wisest of preachers, this is our whole duty -

"Here is the end of the matter; there is nothing more to say. What is the duty laid upon us all? Simply this: fear God, and keep his commandments. And remember that God will bring into judgment your every action, whether hidden or open, good or evil" (Ec 12:13-14).

But let me put it a little differently: we are called to humble submission to divine providence, matched with unshakeable trust in his goodness, and with bold believing prayer for his highest.

---

26   There are many such examples in the Chronicles of the Crusades; ed. Elizabeth Hallam; Weidenfeld and Nicolson, London, 1989. The one above, rejoicing in a Muslim victory is from pg. 312; but the Christians were equally exultant when the fortunes of war happened to go their way.

There is a tension here, as there is in many other parts of scripture, between the need to accept the inevitable and the challenge to believe for the impossible. Both are required of us: sometimes this; sometimes that. But wisdom is available to show us what God wants (Ja 1:5-8).

Chapter Five

THE "CHURCH RELEVANCE" SYNDROME

That same group of pastors mentioned at the beginning of the previous chapter also asked me to address this question: "What issues should be our priority today, so that we can be relevant in today's society?"

My answer: the question is fallacious, if not actually pernicious!

We don't have to be "relevant", only faithful. [27]

We should never feel obliged to justify our presence in the community by doing a set of good works approved by the secular authorities. Whether they want us or not, whether they love us or loathe us, whether they think the church is a blessing or a bane, we are here in obedience to the mandate of Christ, and we will not go away! If a church does decide to set up a school, a soup kitchen, a hostel, a home, or some other welfare agency, it should be for only one reason: "this is what God has told us to do." Projects should not be undertaken because of what another church is doing, nor because the secular authorities expect them, but only because they have been mandated by the Holy Spirit.

THE ABSENT PARSON

Of course, the world would be happier if we just disappeared, or at least quietly minded our own business and left it alone. There is an amusing passage in Thomas Hardy's novel Under The Greenwood Tree. [28] A group of rural parishioners in the village of Mellstock

---

27   For a more detailed discussion of this principle, see my book "Building the Church God Wants."

28   Under The Greenwood Tree; Thomas Hardy; First published in 1872. The quote is from Part One, Chapter Two.

(circa 1830) are lamenting the decease of their former negligent parson, Mr Grinham, who had never bothered them. His replacement was a young and active priest, who was forcing many changes upon the church -

> *"Ay," said Mr Penny, "there was this to be said for (Mr Grinham), that you were quite sure he'd never come mumbudgeting to see ye, just as you were in the middle of your work, and put you out with his fuss and trouble about ye"* . . .
> *"Ah, Mr Grinham was the man!" said Bowman. "Why, he never troubled us wi' a visit from year's end to year's end. You might go anywhere, do anything: you'd be sure never to see him."*
> *"Yes; he was a right sensible pa'son," said Michael. "He never entered our door but once in his life, and that was to tell my poor wife - ay, poor soul, dead and gone now, as we all shall! - that she was such a' old aged person, and lived so far from the church, he didn't at all expect her to come any more to the service."*
> *"And 'a was a very jinerous gentleman about choosing the psalms and hymns o' Sundays. 'Confound ye,' said he, 'blare and scrape what ye will, but don't bother me!'"*

Little has changed since then. "Serve us as we want you to, or leave us alone," is the demand of the world, which we cannot and will not heed.

A LOWLY STATUS

In her delightful Pillow Book, Sei Shonagon, observing life from the Japanese palace a millennium ago, commented on the lowly status of Buddhist priests -

> *"That parents should bring up some beloved son of theirs to be a priest is really distressing. No doubt*

it is an auspicious thing to do; but unfortunately most people are convinced that a priest is as unimportant as a piece of wood, and they treat him accordingly. A priest lives poorly, on meagre food, and cannot even sleep without being criticised. While he is young, it is only natural that he should be curious about all sorts of things, and, if there are women about, he will probably peep in their direction (though, to be sure, with a look of aversion on his face). What is wrong about that? Yet people immediately find fault with him for even so small a lapse." [29]

Again we see that nothing much has changed over the centuries! Here we are in a different culture, with a different faith, yet still the church is under pressure to demonstrate its importance to society. But we have nothing to prove to the world. We are the servants of God, and to our Lord alone we allow ourselves to be answerable.

However, though we may not have to prove ourselves to a godless world, we must certainly demonstrate our credentials before the Lord, and if churches rise and fall it is sometimes because God (not the devil) has acted against them. Long ago Ben Sirach made this observation about nations, which can be applied just as well to the church -

"Empire passes from nation to nation because of injustice, arrogance, and greed" (Sir 10:8).

Churches flourish and fail for the same reasons. The very best, indeed the only, way for us to be "relevant" is to demonstrate in every word and action the gracious love, the incomparable beauty, the gentle humility, and the self-sacrifice of Christ.

---

29   Op. cit. Item #6; pg. 25.

DECISIVE ACTION

According to Thomas Carlyle, one of the most decisive moments in history occurred on October 5th, 1795. On that day, says he, the collapse of the French Revolution began. [30] What happened? The people of Paris were unhappy with the Revolutionary Government, and they marched 40,000 strong to the Tuileries, where the parliament was meeting. They were intent upon taking over the government. Panic seized the legislators, and they turned for rescue to the only experienced military officer who was at hand. His name was Napoleon Bonaparte. The young officer acted swiftly, commandeered a number of cannon, and placed them around the Tuileries. With only a few minutes to spare, he stood waiting for the mob. Carlyle writes -

> *"Now, however, the time is come for it, and the man . . . and the thing we specifically call 'French Revolution' is blown into space by it, and become a thing that was. [31] . . . The Artillery-Officer is steady as bronze; can, if we need, be quick as lightning . . . (the marching throng draws near) . . . Whereupon, thou bronze Artillery-Officer - ? 'Fire!' say the bronze lips. And roar and thunder, roar and again roar, continual, volcano-like . . . go all his great guns. . . . 'It is false,' says Napoleon, 'that we fired first with blank charge; it had been a waste of life to do that.' Most false: the firing was sharp and sharpest shot."*
>
> *"The time was come, and the man" - a man who knew how to ignore the clamour of the mob, and do his duty with unwavering firmness, and with unflinching courage. We need not wonder that he*

---

30   The French Revolution, Book Three, Chapter Seven.

31   This is actually the last sentence in the chapter.

later conquered Europe and crowned himself emperor! [32]

But are we not warriors? Do we not hold the cannon of the Lord in our hand? Are our weapons not mighty enough to pull down every stronghold of the enemy? (2 Co 10:3-5). Are we not called to stretch ever further the borders of our Lord's kingdom?

Every servant of God should have an unshakeable sense of destiny - "This is the time; I am the man" - and a heart to stand bravely, firm and furious for righteousness, set to quench every "fiery dart" hurled by the foe, to defend the church against all attack, and to persevere until we too have been crowned with Christ on the great day of his coronation.

---

32   At his coronation (in 1804) Napoleon snatched the crown out of the hands of the pope, and placed it himself upon his head. It was an act of superb arrogance, an assertion of supremacy over the church, and a moment of great humiliation for the pope (PiusVII).

Chapter Six

THE "INSTITUTIONAL MAINTENANCE" SYNDROME

Resist the pressure toward institutional conformity. We should be proclaimers of the faith, not maintainers of an institution. Yet many pastors are falsely governed by a set of organisational demands. For some, the expectations of a denominational bureaucracy are allowed too much weight, and their ears are deafened to the voice of God. Others are so engrossed with holding onto a complex of local church buildings and departments that they lose sight of the true concerns of the kingdom of God.

Whether denominational or local, beware of institutions!

No doubt our establishments occupy a necessary place in the scheme of things, yet they may also stifle initiative and prevent obedience to the Holy Spirit. Institutions seldom resist the urge to maintain their prerogatives and expand their power. Allow them too much control, and they soon begin to set goals or lay down laws that have little to do with the real work of the ministry.

Nearly all institutions suffer from one great fault: they are innately blind. They have too much privilege to defend to allow any confession of error, too much status to uphold to own any weakness. Consequently, institutions tend to insist on the correctness of their decisions; they cannot admit fallibility, they seldom acknowledge a fault.

Christian organisations must make a special effort to avoid the innate arrogance that belongs to any human structure. A difficult tension exists in the church between the need to be invincible yet at the same time vulnerable! On the one hand, the church must be committed to a strong proclamation of Christ, yet on the other it must also recognise that its knowledge of the gospel is less than perfect (1 Co 13:9, 12). Therefore we should strive for organisational openness, staying vulnerable to criticism, free to learn from others more of the beauty of Christ.

In place of the common urge to build ever higher walls and to fend off all interlopers, Christian institutions, like Christian people, should display a quality of humility. Nowhere in the church is there room for vanity, nor for exclusiveness, nor for any authority that usurps the lordship of Christ.

Yet how rare it is for Christians to be both sternly faithful to their God-given identity and also graciously respectful toward those who differ from them. The sight is so seldom seen, whether corporately or individually, that when such a person is found he or she enters the pages of history:

> *"At Montpellier, Sir Thomas Browne,* [33] *then aged twenty-four, showed himself to be a unique English Protestant. When a (Roman Catholic) religious procession followed the Host or the Crucifix through the streets his compatriots would laugh and jeer. Their conduct brought Browne to tears. He also pitied the penury of the friars. Such feelings were surely unique in a 17th-century Protestant. Even in our time there are people whose religion is measured by hating those who do not agree with them."* [34]

---

33   English physician, author, traveller, and devout Christian (1605-82), whose most renowned work is his "Religio Medici" ("The Faith of a Physician"), which has never been out of print since it was first published in 1643. He was described after his death as "the most imaginative mind since Shakespeare".

34   From the "Introduction" by Halliday Sutherland to Religio Medici, by Sir Thomas Browne; J. M. Dent & Sons Ltd, London, 1956; pg. viii.

THREE COMMON ERRORS

Because we often allow our institutions to assume an inordinate importance we are prone to fall into three errors:

1. We equate ministry with nurture and administration.

Undoubtedly the church should be run well and the people should be shepherded; but those aims must remain secondary to the primary task of ministry (Ac 6:2,4). Many pastors are so busy solving people's problems and managing the programme that they are no longer truly "ministers" of Christ. They have become servants of the congregation and/or slaves to the organisation.

2. In the scramble for statistical success the importance of sound doctrine has been undermined.

Scripture is adamant in its demand that all who minister in the church must be deeply committed both to knowing and proclaiming the true doctrine of Christ (see, for example, Ac 20:26-27; 1 Co 3:10,11; Ep 4:14; 1 Ti 1:3; 4:6; 2 Ti 3:14; 4:1-4; Tit 1:9; 2:1,7-8,15; He 13:9; 2 Jn 1:9). To build a successful organisation, a large congregation, yet leave the people untaught and undiscipled is in the end to fail.

3. The ministry has become "professionalised" -

"Beginning in this century we (pastors) have been following the 'professional model' of ministry. Emulating doctors and lawyers, we act as if we have esoteric training or knowledge unavailable to others, as if seminary is the source of real ministry, as if we are the upper crust of Christianity from whom ministry is meant to trickle down to the lowly laity. This image has debilitated the pastoral ministry, rendered the laity into passive spectators,

and tempted us clergy to seek validation for our work in illegitimate places" [35]

I once felt embarrassed myself because all my theological and ecclesiastical knowledge was attainable by any bright layperson; yet I myself could not hope to master the knowledge of the lawyer, the physician, the mechanic, and other professionals in my congregation. Because of that embarrassment pressure arises to clothe the ministry with a kind of esoteric aura, to demand ever higher educational standards from the clergy. Ordination becomes clothed with a mystique that creates an uncrossable hiatus between pastor and people.

But pastors should gain a sense of value, not by turning themselves into a professional elite, but rather by resting upon two unassailable facts:

> ➤ a sense of divine vocation

> *"The Holy Spirit said, 'Take Barnabas and Saul, and set them apart for me, to do the work to which I have called them.'" (Ac 13:2).*

No one can rightly take the work of the ministry upon himself (cp. He 5:4; Nu 16:5,10,40; Je 14:14-15,21; Jn 3:27). The pastor has a special place in the church, not by reason of superior intelligence, or lofty learning, or professional skill, but solely because he or she is called by God to a task that cannot be fulfilled without a divine commission.

> ➤ a recognition of divine purpose

Paul lists five ministry-gifts (Ep 4:11), and gives them all one supreme purpose: they must achieve nothing less than "equipping the saints to do the work of ministry" (vs. 12). We ministers have the actual job of training others to do our job! But here is the secret: none of us is adequate for that task, nor can anyone be truly furnished for it, except by the call and gift of God. Whatever other

---

35   William H. Willimon in "The Christian Ministry" (Nov/Dec 1992); pg. 39.

training, education, or provision, is added to the minister's call must always remain ancillary to it; nor can any other qualification be accepted as a substitute for it. Any Christian leader who knows that he or she has a God-given vocation, and knows that only someone ordained by God can properly "equip the saints for the work of the ministry", should be rid of any absurd feelings of inferiority! Even if there are many highly competent professionals in the church, the head of a God-called, God-anointed pastor should remain unbowed.

> *"You should teach these things with authority, urging and contending for them; and don't allow anyone to look down on you" (Tit 2:15).*

Chapter Seven

THE
"PERSONAL IMPORTANCE" SYNDROME

Lady Windermere: Why do you talk so trivially about life?

Lord Darlington: Because I think that life is far too important a thing ever to talk seriously about it. [36]

> *"In this world there are only two tragedies. One is not getting what one wants, and the other is getting it. The last is much the worse; the last is a real tragedy."* [37]

Only two things can be done with life: one must either weep, or laugh. The second is the only sensible choice. God is laughing (Ps 2:4a), so I might as well join him!

Yet how can we laugh in the face of so much pain? Jesus used one noun to express all the misery Satan has brought upon men and women: he called him the "Thief". [38] What sorrow is not found there? Theft is the common pain, the burning grief of us all. We are robbed of our holiness and happiness, of our health and prosperity, of our love and our laughter, of our dreams and our destiny. No one escapes this depredation; and God's children, who understand more finely what life should be, feel the loss more keenly. [39]

---

36   Oscar Wilde, Lady Windermere's Fan, Act One.

37   Ibid. Act Three; spoken by Mr Dumby to Lord Darlington.

38   John 10:10.

39   This paragraph and those that follow, to the first heading, are taken from my book "Discovery", Chapter Four.

Which of us, starting on the pilgrim path, has not dreamed wonderful dreams of empires wrought, castles built, dragons defeated, fabulous deeds done for the glory of God? Yet at the end of the journey, how petty the done seems against the immensity of the undone; how dismal the present seems against the radiant light of yesterday's hopes! No hand has ever built all that the mind imagined; no heart has ever dared all that it has dreamed; no action has ever equalled the aspirations that drove it; no zeal has ever fully overcome the leaden weight of the flesh. Amid the sweetest fortune and favour of this life there is always a timbre of grief. Love remains debtor to its promised joy; ashes embitter the taste of ambition's fulfilment; happiness crumbles beneath the shadow of mortality; the grave digs a mocking end to every earthly pretension.

Suddenly, just as despair begins to chill the soul, faith hears another voice. It cries: Satan can rob you only on the surface! The Thief carries off only life's pebbles! Your real treasure lies where no bandit can touch it, nor moth consume, nor rust corrupt! [40]

That is why Paul wrote -

> *"Since you have been lifted out of death with Christ, turn your eyes toward heaven, for Christ is there, sitting at God's right hand. Fix your minds on that higher plane, not down here on earth. Surely you understand this? You began by dying with Christ, and now your life is hidden with Christ in God. When Christ, who is our true life, suddenly appears, then you too will appear with him, clothed in the same glory!"* [41]

Do you understand those things? If you do, then you really won't care very much what happens to you during the short span of your

---

40   Luke 12:33.

41   Colossians 3:1-4.

mortal life. Your lasting happiness finds its home beyond time in eternity, and beyond earth in heaven.

Nonetheless, although such ideas are written boldly in scripture, people keep on making the same mistakes -

RESENTING THE POTTER

"Contentment with godliness," said Paul, "is great gain" (1 Ti 6:6); yet often the most discontented person in a local church is its pastor! How frustrated so many shepherds are, because their ministry seems to be locked into mediocrity. But (as even pagan thinkers have realised) we need to be cheerful about the way God has ordered our lives -
"Do not indulge in dreams of having what you have not, but reckon up the chief of the blessings you do possess, and then thankfully remember how you would crave for them if they were not yours. At the same time, however, beware lest delight in them leads you to cherish them so dearly that their loss would destroy your peace of mind." [42]

As Publilius Syrus said (circa 100 B.C.) -

"Whatever you can lose, you should reckon of no account!"

I see no reason to suppose that pastors alone are exempt from that piece of wisdom. Any pastor can lose his church. It can be taken from him by congregational revolt, by the collapse of his health, by denominational fiat, by Satanic attack, by decision of the local board, or any one of several other misfortunes. Even if you keep for many years what you have built, still time or the grave will eventually take it from you. Every church, even the finest, must

---

42   The Roman emperor Marcus Aurelius (121-180), admonishing himself in his personal diary. The Meditations of Marcus Aurelius; tr. by Maxwell Staniforth; Penguin Books, 1986.

eventually crumble back into dust. Paul's contemporary, the Roman philosopher and statesman Seneca, once found in his children an illustration of the ephemerality of all human works -

"Our love for our (children) [43] . . . should be tempered by the reflection that we have been given no guarantee of their immortality, or even of their longevity. We need constantly to remind ourselves to bestow on them our love as upon possessions destined to vanish, or indeed already vanishing from our sight. . . . Enjoy by all means the company of your children while you can, and in turn give them the enjoyment of your society. . . .

> *"Tonight is not to be depended on; no, that is too great an allowance - this hour is not to be depended on. Make haste; you are being pursued; this fellowship will soon be broken up; this happy companionship must come to an end, its noisy gaiety be silenced. Destruction is the universal law; do you not know, poor mortals, that life is a race to dissolution?"* [44]

Therefore, sensible spiritual leaders keep a light touch on their ministry. Today you have it; tomorrow you may not! Pragmatic people hold hard only to those things that are important, they put lasting value only on what cannot be taken away from them.

How can you assess what is important?

Suppose you were a Protestant pastor in 17th century France, condemned because of your faith to be chained to the oar of a slave galley for the rest of your life - what then would truly matter to you?

---

43   If you are a pastor, apply this also to your spiritual children, the members of your congregation.

44   Seneca: Four Tragedies and Octavia; tr. by E. F. Watling; Penguin Classics, 1970; pg. 313-314. The passage quoted above comes from Seneca's prose work "Ad Marciam", Section Ten.

"We went to visit the Galleys, being about 25; the Captaine of the Galley Royal gave us most courteous entertainment in his cabine, the slaves in the interim playing both loud and soft musiq very rarely. [45] *Then he shew'd us how he commanded their motions with a nod and his whistle, making them row out. The spectacle was to me new and strange, to see so many hundreds of miserably naked persons, having their heads shaven close and having onely high red bonnets, a payre of coarse canvas drawers, their whole backs and leggs naked, doubly chayned about their middle and leggs, in couples, and made fast to their seates, and all commanded in a trise by an imperious and cruell seaman. . . .*

"I was amaz'd to contemplate how these miserable catyfs [46] *lie in their galley crowded together . . . Their rising forward and falling back at their oare is a miserable spectacle, and the noyse of their chaines with the roaring of the beaten waters has something of the strange and fearfull to one unaccustom'd to it. They are rul'd and chastiz'd by strokes on their backs and soles of their feete on the least disorder, and without the least humanity . . .* [47]

---

45   That is, skilfully.

46   A captive, particularly one confined in a state of misery and pain.

47   The Grand Tour: 1592-1796; ed. by Roger Hudson; Folio Society, London, 1993; pg. 65. The above account is by the 17th cent. English diarist John Evelyn, who went on the Grand Tour between the years 1643-47. While on tour he visited the harbour of Marseilles, where there were a number of galleys moored. They remained a tourist attraction for another 100 years, until galleys were finally phased out of the French fleet (the last European navy to do so).

Across several centuries, thousands of Christian men, young and old, including many pastors, were condemned to the galleys of France and Spain, where they died wretchedly, still chained to their oars. If they had ever hoped to achieve greatness, they now had to find it within their own spirits, for their outer environment was an unending torrent of pain. The unfailing "goodness and mercy" of God had to find a different expression for them, channelled somehow through their chains, and the lash, and pitiless hours of relentless toil. Their persecutors had indeed stripped from them everything that a man can lose. They kept only what cannot be stolen: their devotion to Christ.

Their suffering was magnified by a terrible temptation. Any galley slave who renounced his faith and embraced the creed of his tormentors was at once released. Surprisingly few accepted the offer. Although threatened by years of torment more awful than we can imagine, still they held firm, and built a spiritual empire within greater than any of the kingdoms wrought by history's famous conquerors! (Pr 16:32; 25:28).

Beware of Ambition

Ambition is admirable, if it is confined to discovering what God wants and doing it. But there is another kind of ambition, antagonistic to the divine purpose, ruinous in its effect, which sages have often railed against. For example, two hundred years before Christ was born, an old Jewish rabbi who was then about 80-years old, gave this advice to his young disciples -

> *"Do not ask the Lord to give you some high office, nor even the king to promote you. . . . Do not yearn to be a judge, for you may not be strong enough to root out injustice. Why would you risk being overawed by the powerful, and so ruin your integrity?"* [48]

---

48   Sirach 7:4-7

Or if you prefer something canonical, then listen to Solomon -

> *"Why do you wear yourself out trying to get rich?*
> *Have the good sense to stop now! As soon as your*
> *eye is fixed on some treasure, away it will fly!*
> *Suddenly your fortune will sprout wings and soar*
> *off into the distant clouds like an eagle ... You*
> *know it is foolish to eat too much honey; surely then*
> *you realise that only sickness can result if you keep*
> *trying to pile honour on top of honour. ... You*
> *would do better to chase the wind than to keep on*
> *toiling hard to fill both hands when you could fill*
> *one hand with peace of mind!"* [49]

Let me paraphrase that counsel a little: "Why do you wear yourself out trying to be successful? No sooner have you won your prize than away it will fly!" [50] Solomon and Sirach both mean this: be cautious about hungering for position and power; be wary of preferment; don't be too anxious for outward success or honour. Promotion to a position above his capacity has destroyed many a good man. Are you sure you can handle the office you desire? You may be a fine shepherd of a flock of one hundred souls; but two hundred could break your spirit. Let God thrust you as high as he pleases - and you must be willing to follow wherever he leads - but only a fool begins something he cannot finish (Lu 14:28-30).

Jesus taught the same lesson of contentment with the Father's providence in Matthew 6:25-34; and remember again the sharp saying, "When Jesus saw the crowds, he went up a mountain!" (5:1). Like the Master, we should recognise the great peril that hides in any craving for bigness, or worse, for popularity. We dare

---

49   Proverbs 23:4-5; 25:27; Ecclesiastes 4:6.

50   "Successful", of course, here means striving for success in a merely statistical sense; that is, someone yearning to gather a bigger crowd, or to earn more money, or to gain a higher position, and the like. It does not refer to the "success" that every Christian must crave, of doing all that God wants, and of being all that God commands.

not embrace the world's concept of prosperity. For us Christians there can be only one way to define "success": discover what God wants, and do it! For some, that will mean vast achievement; for others (in the reckoning of the world), obscurity. What does it matter, so long as God is pleased? To be acclaimed by the world but scorned by the Father is poor gain; while if the Father approves me, what value can any other opinion hold?

Paul too takes up the theme in 1 Timothy 6:6-10, which echoes, and in some phrases quotes, the wisdom of Sirach -

> *"The only necessary things in life are water, bread, and clothing, along with a home to allow you some privacy. .... Learn how to be content, whether you have much or little... You will never be right in God's sight if you yearn to be rich; chase after money and you will soon be lost. Gold has been the ruin of many; those who crave it will find themselves face to face with destruction.... Happy indeed are rich people who stay blameless, who have not let gold become their god. Do such people actually exist? If you can find them, bring them here so that we may praise them! They have achieved a stunning miracle!" (29:21-23; 31:5-11).*

But answer this: were Jesus, and Paul, and Solomon and Sirach before them, talking about "gold" only in its narrow fiscal sense? Or should we rather understand them to mean whatever each person calls wealth? For one person, riches means much money, while another finds wealth in worldly honour. The "gold" a preacher chases may be a large congregation - not money in the bank, but bodies in the pews. Some preachers run after a crowd more avidly than any pirate ever lusted for treasure. I see no real difference between the craving of either of them, nor in the goals they so fervently pursue.

Try this experiment: go back over the passages mentioned above (from Proverbs, Sirach, Matthew, and Timothy), and wherever you read "gold" or its equivalent, read instead "success". [51] You may be startled by a sobering impact upon your notion of how well your motives conform to the standards set by the Father!

Over-reaching ambition has always been called an evil thing by thoughtful people -

> *" . . . I think that in practical life there is something about success, actual success, that is a little unscrupulous, something about ambition that is unscrupulous always. Once a man has set his heart and soul on getting to a certain point, if he has to climb the crag, he climbs the crag; if he has to walk in the mire, he walks in the mire."* [52]

Many ambitious preachers, who began well scaling the craggy heights heavenward, has been later found wallowing in the mire of compromise - willing to do anything that has to be done to fulfil their earth-focussed goals.

> *"I entered the main street of the place, . . . (and there) a little dog, in mad terror was rushing past; for some human imps had tied a tin-kettle to its tail; thus did the agonised creature, loud-jingling, career through the whole length of the Borough, and become notable enough. Fit emblem of many a Conquering Hero, to whom Fate (wedding Fantasy to Sense, as it often elsewhere does) has malignantly appended a tin-kettle of Ambition, to chase*

---

51   Remember that I am using "success" here, not in the sense of doing the Father's will, but of earthly, statistical, achievement - more money, more honour, bigger crowd, larger building, and the like.

52   From Oscar Wilde's play, An Ideal Husband Act Two. The speaker is Lord Goring.

*him on; which the faster he runs, urges him the
faster, the more loudly, and the more foolishly."* [53]

Every Christian should of course be moved by the vision of God
(Ph 3:12-14); just beware that your vision does not decay into
ambition, and instead of leading you upward to glory becomes a
snare to your soul.

Think Soberly

Paul warns us to think soberly about ourselves, neither estimating
ourselves too high nor too low, but with an honest reckoning (Ro
12:3). He may have been echoing another passage from Sirach -

> *"My son, keep a balance between self-esteem and
> modesty. Learn how to prize yourself according to
> your true worth. Who will speak up for you if you
> never stop talking yourself down? Who will honour
> you if you keep on dishonouring yourself?" (10:28-
> 29)*

Happy are those who neither love nor loathe themselves too much,
but are content with what God has made them and given them (Ro
9:20-21). Such people also avoid like a pestilence the folly of
taking either themselves or life too seriously. Here is a worthy
aphorism: so long as you can laugh at yourself you will never
suffer a breakdown!

> *Then let us mock with ancient mirth this comic,
> cosmic plan;
> The stars are laughing at the earth; God's greatest
> joke is man.
> For laughter is a buckler bright, and scorn a
> shining spear;*

---

53 Thomas Carlyle (1795-1881) in Sartor Resartus, Book Two, Section
Three.

So let us laugh with all our might at folly, fraud, and fear.
Yet on our sorry selves be spent our most sardonic glee;
Oh don't pay life the compliment to take it seriously.
For he who can himself despise, be surgeon to the bone,
May win to worth in other's eyes, to wisdom in his own! [54]

Oscar Wilde's paradox - "life is far too important a thing ever to talk seriously about it" - is more true than most people want to believe. Part of the problem with the church is that Christians have a view of themselves and their mission that is much too inflated. The Lord could actually do quite well without any of us! Any time he wants more servants, or more worshippers, he has only to stir up a few pebbles -

> *"I tell you that God can make as many children as he wants out of these stones!" (Mt 3:9).*

Shall we then treat life and ministry flippantly? God forbid! We are engaged in the noblest task in the world; we are about the King's business! Yet the task is so immense, and we are so inadequate, that the only sensible thing to do is laugh! What concord can heaven have with earth, or the spiritual with the natural, or the infinite with the finite? Here is God's joke: "we hold heaven's treasure in a clay pot!" (2 Co 4:7). The church is preposterous to the point of absurdity. Yet just because of that, it also represents God's highest wisdom. So we must work hard, yet always with good humour. Our task is royal, yet we remain ridiculous! Even Jesus mixed hilarity with the darkest hours of life-

> *"How happy you should be when you suffer insults, and beatings, and every kind of slander for my sake.*

---

54   Robert Service, Laughter, stanza three.

You should exult and go wild with joy, for your reward in heaven will be enormous!" (Mt 5:12)

When he found his disciples filled with happiness for the wrong reason (because their ministry had been successful), he rebuked them! (Lu 10:20). He knew well enough that they would not always succeed as preachers; but there was no reason why they should ever fail as Christians. Earthly triumphs may wax and wane, but the inscribing of our names in heaven remains sure for ever! So we must learn this secret: in the midst of our most earnest labours to bubble with laughter. While we view our work with the utmost seriousness, yet we must also pronounce it both impossible, and therefore ludicrous.

When Herman Melville was working on his masterpiece, Moby Dick, he became deeply conscious of its shortcomings. He reached a point in writing the novel when he realised that the vision that drove him would not be fulfilled. Like a man whose eye is fixed on a bright star, his vision reached where his feet could not carry him. He despaired even of catching a shadow of his dream: "I promise nothing complete; because any human thing supposed to be complete, must for that very reason infallibly be faulty."

Whales were his theme; and of it he said -

> *"It is a ponderous task; no ordinary letter-sorter in the Post Office [55] is equal to it. To grope down into the bottom of the sea after them; [56] to have one's hands among the unspeakable foundations, ribs, and very pelvis of the world; this is a fearful thing. What am I that should essay to hook the nose of this Leviathan! The tauntings in Job might well appal me: 'Will he (Leviathan) make a covenant with thee? Behold, the hope of him is vain!' ... (So I*

---

55   He began his working life in a bank, and spent his last twenty years as an officer in the New York customs service.

56   We are even more absurd, for we try to scale the heights of heaven!

must leave my task) unfinished, even as the great Cathedral of Cologne was left, with the crane still standing upon the top of the uncompleted tower. For small erections may be finished by their first architects; grand ones, true ones, ever leave the copestone to posterity. God keep me from ever completing anything. This whole book is but a draught - nay, but the draught of a draught. Oh, Time, Strength, Cash, and Patience!" [57]

Call your task then, at once the silliest and the sanest any person has undertaken. If you are tempted to get careless, remind yourself how important your work is; if you become proud, or unduly solemn, call yourself a clown. In any case, develop the art of standing apart from life from time to time, view yourself objectively, see how comical it all is, and share the Father's amusement. You will live longer and happier, for it is still true that "a merry heart is better than a dose of medicine!" (Pr 17:22; and see also 15:13-15).

---

57 From Chapter 32. What Melville felt about his labours, any godly writer, any true preacher, must feel - how short of the dream the production falls. Never enough time, or strength, or money, or skill! We are burdened with a task that must be done, yet we are children struggling to do a man's, nay an angel's, work! Melville is also a classic example of unrealised hopes. Although he is now renowned as one of America's greatest writers, in his own lifetime he failed to gain the audience he desired. He died in obscurity, poor, and deeply despondent.

Chapter Eight

THE "BUSY MARTHA" SYNDROME

"Do not lift a weight that is too heavy for you, or try to make yourself the equal of those who are greater and richer than you are" (Sir 13:2).

You can stretch only so high; you can lift only so much. Anyone who tries to lift a weight that is too heavy will either be crushed by it, or humiliated when it slips out their hands. So too, you can only reach so high. Stretch too far and you will topple over. Which brings us to three problems closely akin to the syndrome discussed in the previous chapter -

REACHING TOO HIGH

In the last two lines of Act Five of "Oedipus", by Seneca, the Chorus sings the words -

Whenever man exceeds the mean
He stands upon the brink of danger!

Similarly, Thoreau wrote -

"All the world reposes in beauty to him who preserves equipoise in his life, and moves serenely on his path without secret violence; as he who sails down a stream, he has only to steer, keeping his bark in the middle, and carry it around the falls." [58]
"In me there dwells
No greatness, save it be some far-off touch

---

58 Op. cit. pg. 260. See also the last footnote in the next chapter.

Of greatness to know well I am not great." [59]

Thus those who are wise will first know themselves and be content with what they know. Then they will work happily within their own proper boundaries. When God wants someone to be a spiritual weight-lifter he gives him the muscles for it. No matter how much a lifter may exercise and train, he cannot go beyond his physical limits. Nature itself imposes a maximum load. The same is true in the church.

RESISTING THE TIDE

Scripture speaks forcefully about the uncertainties of life, and good planning takes account of these vicissitudes (Ja 4:14-16; Ec 9:1,11-12; 11:6). The wise are prepared alike for fortune and misfortune. Here also the good sense of scripture has been often confirmed -

> *Thus fell the famous, mighty Hercules!*
> *Who then may trust the dice, at Fortune's throw?*
> *Who joins in worldly struggles such as these*
> *Will be, when least prepared for it, laid low!*
> *Wise is the man who well has learnt to know*
> *Himself. Beware! When Fortune would elect*
> *To trick a man, she plots his overthrow*
> *By such a means as he would least expect.* [60]

> *Even a pirate was aware of life's chancy path -*

---

59   From Tennyson's Idylls of the King, "Lancelot and Elaine", line 447.

60   Geoffrey Chaucer (1345-1400), Canterbury Tales - "The Monk's Tale - `Hercules' "; tr. Nevill Coghill; Penguin Classics, 1977; pg. 211. In the Tale, Hercules, the Greek hero renowned for his "Twelve Labours", was given a poisoned shirt by a woman. Rather than perish at a woman's hand, he took his own life by "raking burning coals upon himself until he died". The Monk told a series of stories, all with the same moral: fortune and fame remain uncertain even for the best and greatest of mortals.

"The lives of men are at the mercy of the slenderest chances. A whole destiny may be influenced by no more than the set of the wind at a given moment." [61]

Those whose ships were driven by the wind knew how much their destiny depended upon forces over which they had no control. Perhaps we, in an age of power-driven vessels, have become complacent, and think that we are now altogether masters of our own fate. All who think so cannot but hurt themselves.

One of the Royal Scenes displayed in the Royal Clock on the top floor of the Queen Victoria Building, in Sydney, is "King Canute Stopping the Waves in 1033." [62] Like the ancient monarch, those who are wise understand that the shifting tides of life cannot be prevented. Canute knew that he could not stop the foaming sea from rushing upon him. Why then did he try? Wearied by the incessant flattery of his courtiers, the king told them to carry his throne down to the beach and place it in the path of the advancing waves. As the waters came toward him, the king ordered them to recede again. Heedless of his royal command, the waves rolled on relentlessly. He sat there calmly as the sea rose around his throne, until his worried courtiers hastily rescued him.

Afterward, Canute admonished the assembled lords and ladies. He bade them to remember the futility of earthly glory, and that he was but a man. He rebuked their empty flatteries, and told them to

---

61   Rafael Sabatini op. cit., Chapter One, "The Blank Shot".

62   Beginning as king of the Danes, by the year 1016, when he was only 22 years old, Canute had battled his way also to the crown of England. He spent the remainder of his life in England, reigning over the entire land south of the Scottish border. For the first two years after his English crowning he consolidated his throne with great savagery, but then, with his kingdom now secure, his character underwent an astonishing change. He became a devout, wise, temperate, and law-abiding ruler, who displayed a high concept of the duties of a monarch. He restored equal rights to all citizens, vastly improved the administration of the realm, was liberal to the churches and monasteries, and encouraged the conversion to Christianity of the people (many of whom were still pagan).

conduct themselves with greater humility. Then, according to the ancient Chronicle, the king took off his crown, placed it upon the head of a statue of the crucified Christ, and never again wore it himself.

What Goes Out, Comes Back!

Should we then be pessimistic, expecting the worst rather than the best? How foolish! Remember that whichever way the tide flows, it must sooner or later reverse itself! Divine providence does not always topple those who are standing tall. Indeed, the Lord just as often takes people from a low estate and raises them to the most dizzying heights (Ec 4:13-14). This too was recognised by Chaucer; for after the Monk had told a long series of gloomy stories about famous people whose lives were overtaken by ruin, his companions began to protest -

> *"Ho, my good sir, no more!" exclaimed the Knight.*
> *"What you have said so far no doubt is right,*
> *And more than right, but still a little grief*
> *Will do for most of us, in my belief.*
> *As for myself, I take great displeasure*
> *In tales of those who once knew wealth and leisure*
> *And then are felled by some unlucky hit.*
> *But it's a joy to hear the opposite,*
> *For instance tales of men of low estate*
> *Who climb aloft and growing fortunate*
> *Remain secure in their prosperity;*
> *That is delightful as it seems to me*
> *And is a proper tale to tell."* [63]
>
> *Similarly, Seneca wrote -*
> *Kings of the earth must bow to a higher kingdom.*
> *Some, whom the rising sun sees highly exalted,*
> *The same sun may see fallen at its departing.*

63   Ibid. pg. 231.

No man should put his trust in the smile of fortune,
No man abandon hope in the time of trouble . . .
Under God's hand, life's circle is ever revolving,
The swift wheel turning. [64]

Good counsel! Neither put too much "trust in the smile of fortune" nor ever "abandon hope in the time of trouble"! Although today's green pastures may become tomorrow's valley of death, yet the psalmist expected to come safely through that valley. Nothing could still his song: "God's goodness and mercy will follow me all the days of my life".

There is never an excuse for becoming negative, sour, parsimonious; rather, we who believe should stay full of high expectations, both from ourselves and from God. We may quote the pirate again -

"Fortune," Captain Blood was wont to say, "detests
a niggard. Her favours are reserved for the man
who knows how to spend nobly and to stake
boldly!" [65]

RELIEVING THE URGENT

Don't be controlled by the important or the urgent, or by anything in the world, but only by the Father's purpose. You cannot solve every person's problems, nor should you try to do so (cp. Lu 12:13-15). Consider all the political, social, and cultural evils that Jesus could have addressed, but which he resolutely ignored. His ministry remained narrowly focussed, he stuck to the programme of God for his life. Scripture says that he had but one commitment: "Here I am, just as it is written of me in the scroll. I have come, O God, to do your will" (He 10:7). He said,

---

64 From the play Thyestes, Act Three, the final Chorus; tr. by E. F. Watling, op. cit., pg. 71-72.

65 The Fortunes of Captain Blood, by Rafael Sabatini; Pan Books, London, 1963; pg. 62; (Ep. III).

"I can do nothing by myself. I can do only what I see the Father doing. Whatever the Father does, that is what the Son does. ... I cannot act by myself. ... I do not seek to do my own will, but only the will of him who sent me. ... I do not speak out of my own authority, because the Father who sent me has told me himself what to say and how to say it. ... So long as daylight lasts I must continue to do the work of the One who sent me" (Jn 5:19,30; 12:49; 9:4).

Jesus did only what the Father told him to do; he said only what the Father told him to say. He said "yes" to God, but "no" to everyone else. Perhaps there is no more important word for some Christian leaders and workers to learn, than how to say "No!" - winsomely, graciously, kindly, sympathetically, but nonetheless firmly, "No!" Others will insist that the task is urgent, or necessary, or important, that there is no-one else to do it except you, that untold harm will follow if you don't rush into the breach, that you absolutely must say "Yes!" But unless the burden is one that God himself has told you carry, still you should say, "No!"

Between "yes" and "no" lies a choice that will either put you on or lead you off the path to success in fulfilling the Father's purpose for your life.

Chapter Nine

THE "WRONG CALL"

SYNDROME

Text: "We recommend ourselves to you by our pure behaviour, sound doctrine, patience and kindness, gifts of the Holy Spirit, genuine love, proclamation of the truth, and by the power of God" (2 Co 6:6-7).

Seldom would a visiting preacher today be commended to a city in the terms Paul used. His focus differed from ours. We major on achievement, Paul preferred to look at character. I do not mean that what you do is unimportant, but that great deeds mean nothing unless they arise out of a great character (1 Co 13:1-3). Why do we so often get it so wrong? Perhaps because we have misunderstood the nature of the ministry. This chapter explores four expressions of the local pastor's role, and the next looks at the proper focus for Christian leaders.

THE GIFTED PASTOR

Some pastors are highly gifted, vigorous, energetic, and their churches inevitably grow. They are persuasive speakers, charismatic leaders, good motivators, and display tough management qualities. Whatever career or profession they may choose to embark upon, they are people born for great success.

"Men of genius do not excel in any profession because they labour in it, but they labour in it because they excel" [66]
"Genius must be born, and never can be taught" [67]

---

66   William Hazlitt (1778-1830); Characteristics #416.

If I may use David's "mighty men" as an analogy, then these pastors would deserve to be ranked with "The Three". They would be the top commanders and warriors in the army of Israel (1 Ch 11:11). So too in the church, they are its most gifted leaders, with few peers. I have little to say about them in this book, because they hardly need to be told how to fulfil their ministry. Their innate sense of destiny will carry them on into successful fulfilment of the Father's purpose.

Such people should be honoured for the work they do, for the gift of God that is in them, and for their importance in the expansion of the kingdom. They need much prayer, for they are prime targets for the enemy's "fiery darts". Their triumphs lift the entire church, their defeats bring shame upon all.

Of them we may echo the eulogy of Sirach -

> *"Let us now sing the praise of famous men . . . for the Lord ordained them to great glory, and from the beginning appointed them to show his majesty. Some of them gained empires and became renowned because of their astonishing exploits. Others were far-seeing men, shrewd and intelligent, whose words were the oracles of God in the land"* *(44:1-3).*

THE CAPABLE PASTOR

These are leaders whose churches will grow if they augment their abilities by gathering around them other well-gifted people (as Jesus said the rascally steward should have done, Mt 25:27). They too (like the first group) have strong leadership and motivational qualities, but must compensate for the lack of certain skills.

The difference between these leaders and those in the first group is the difference between genius and talent:

---

67   John Dryden (1631-1700).

Talk not of genius baffled.
Genius is the master of man.
Genius does what it must,
And talent does what it can. [68]

"Talent is that which is in a man's power; genius is
that in whose power a man is." [69]

I have often thought that of all possible states, this must be the most painful. The talented are near enough to the brilliant to know the meaning of true excellence, and yet realise also that they will never achieve it. They are clever enough to know they are not clever enough! But people of lesser skill, having little comprehension of what genius entails, also lack any envy of it. Here is a man who can hardly pick out a simple melody on the piano. He may admire a keyboard virtuoso but will hardly feel stung by the musical gulf that separates them. Here is another man whose talent is high, and who devotes endless hours to practice, yet always falls just short of concert ability. What infinite anguish he will suffer because of the small gap that divides him from the genius!

"Mediocrity knows nothing higher than itself, but
talent instantly recognises genius" [70] *- and what*
pain that recognition can cause! [71]

---

68   From The Last Words of a Sensitive Poet, by Lord Lytton (1803-73). Within his lifetime Lytton was an immensely popular novelist and poet. But toward the end of his life he realised that he had failed to reach the heights of literary achievement (especially in poetry) of which he had once dreamed. He died with his noblest hopes disappointed

69   James Russell Lowell (1819-1891).

70   Sir Arthur Conan Doyle (1859-1930); The Valley of Fear.

71   If you have seen the film "Amadeus" you may understand what this means. The film ostensibly portrays the life of Mozart; in reality, it deals with the pain the talented suffer in the presence of the brilliant. Salieri (Mozart's adversary in the film) was the leading composer and musician in Vienna until Mozart arrived and utterly eclipsed him. The film explores Salieri's

Unfair as it may seem (and life is seldom fair) the top group of pastors will succeed almost despite themselves; they can hardly help but do gloriously; their triumph appears almost inevitable. But the second group, the talented pastors, though they are highly skilled, must work harder to achieve their goals. Even then they cannot equal the exploits of genius. They are clever enough to stand among the leaders of David's "Thirty Mighty Men", but they cannot rise to the skill of "The Three" (1 Ch 11:20-21, 25).

Sirach would have put these skilled leaders in the second rank of his "famous men" -

> *"There were those who guided the people by their shrewd counsel, who shared their deep knowledge of the nation's law, whose teaching was always guided by wisdom. Some also composed lovely music, while others wrote sacred poetry" (vs. 4-5).*

THE COMPETENT PASTOR

Here we meet leaders who are well-gifted in two or three areas, but have other traits of personality or temperament that tend to undermine their efforts. Unless they learn how to isolate those traits, or compensate for them in some way, they will never achieve their full ministry-potential. These leaders would be fit to join David's company of "Thirty Mighty Men", but not to command the company, nor can they ever rise to the level of "The Three" (2 Sa 23:24-38).

They would deserve Sirach's third-level encomium -

> *"Some were endowed with wealth and strength, able to secure their homes in peace and prosperity; they won high praise from their fellow citizens, and were held in honour by all who knew them. Some of them*

---

failure to cope with this overshadowing. His despair finally led him to incarceration in a mental asylum.

have even left behind them a name; they are not forgotten, but will be long remembered" (vs. 6-8).

THE AVERAGE PASTOR

Now we are among the majority of pastors and local church leaders. Here is where most of us stand. Such leaders would be fit to rank with the lesser officers, the small company commanders, of David's army, but they cannot aspire to "The Thirty" nor to "The Three". Let us note at once that average pastors build average churches; that is a law of life. Does this mean that such leaders should be ashamed of lacking high skills? Nonsense! Every army, as the military proverb has it, runs on its sergeants! Notice what honour such captains were given in David's army. These men were not to be despised, for they too were esteemed as -

> *"...powerful fighters who helped him in war; they were archers who could shoot arrows and sling stones with either their right hand or their left . . . they were tough and experienced warriors, experts in handling either the shield or the spear, with the courage and ferocity of lions, swift as a deer upon the mountains . . . the least of them was equal to a hundred and the greatest to a thousand!" (1 Ch 12:1-2, 8, 14).*

Likewise, Sirach includes these among his "famous men". They may be unsung by the world, and sometimes even by the church; yet they deserve to be highly honoured -

> "Let us now sing the praises of famous men . . . although some of them are now forgotten. All memory of them died when they died; they have become as if they had never been born . . . But they too were godly men, whose deeds have not been forgotten, because they left wealth behind them to be shared among their descendants. . . . Their offspring will go on increasing, and their glory will

never perish. Their bodies lie peacefully in the grave, but their fame cannot die, because the assembly is indebted to their wisdom, and the congregation will sing their praise!" (vs. 9-15)

Safety On The Plain

If you are among this average majority, you might rather be glad of it, not disappointed nor frustrated. History abounds with examples of the perils that confront men and women who possess exalted skill. Consider Andrea del Sarto, an early 16th century Italian artist, whose talent was so immense, and his style so impeccable, he was known as "the faultless painter". Yet because painting was so easy for him, his work lacked fire. Robert Browning describes him in his dramatic monologue, Andrea del Sarto, and causes the artist to speak enviously about less-gifted painters. Sarto realised that the toiling artisan, though possessed only average skill, would experience more of the zest of life than the genius would ever enjoy -

> *There burns a truer light in them,*
> *In their vexed, beating, stuffed and stopped-up brain,*
> *Heart, or whate'er else, than goes on to prompt*
> *This low-pulsed forthright craftsman's hand of mine.*
> *Their work drops groundward, but themselves, I know,*
> *Reach many a time a heaven that's shut to me . . .*
> *Ah, but a man's reach should exceed his grasp,*
> *Or what's a heaven for? all is silver-grey*
> *Placid and perfect with my art - the worse!* [72]

---

72   Sub-titled "The Faultless Painter". Browning's poem is based upon a 1550 work, "Lives of the Great Painters, Sculptors, and Architects", by Georgio Vasari (1511-1574). In it Vasari writes: "We have now come, after the lives of so many craftsmen who have been outstanding, some for

When you have less you try harder. There is a noble adventure to be joined when "a man's reach exceeds his grasp". While the toil of ordinary workmen often "drops groundward", they themselves "reach many times a heaven that's shut" to the prodigy. They feel a passion, they know a drive, they attempt a mountain, they run for a prize, which familiarity has dulled for those who do everything easily. The same bag of money that means nothing to a millionaire brings inexpressible joy to a poor man.

> *"Yesterday I finished my tenth ballad. When I have done about a score I will seek a publisher. If I cannot find one, I will earn, beg, or steal the money to get them printed. Then, if they do not sell, I will hawk them from door to door. Oh, I'll succeed, I know I'll succeed. And yet I don't want an easy success; give me the joy of the fight, the thrill of the adventure."* [73]

God is debtor to no one. When he gives much of one thing he takes away another. If there are joys known only by the wealthy,

---

colouring, some for drawing, and others for invention, to the most excellent Andrea del Sarto, in whose single person nature and art showed all that painting can achieve by means of drawing, colouring, and invention . . . (His) figures, despite their simplicity and purity, were well-conceived, without errors, and in all respects utterly perfect ... rare and truly inspired . . . (In his 'Last Supper' Sarto used) so good a style that this work was held to be, as it certainly is, the most smooth, the most vivacious in colouring and drawing that he ever did, or rather, that anyone could do. For apart from all the rest, he gave such infinite grace, grandeur, and majesty to all the figures that I do not know how to praise his (painting) without saying too little, it being so fine that whoever sees it is stupefied." Yet in the end Vasari has to say: "Andrea displayed poor spirit in the actions of his life, and contented himself with very little . . . (although) in the art of painting he (possessed) enormous talent." (Lives of the Artists in Three Volumes, by Georgio Vasari; tr. by George Bull; Folio Society, London, 1993; Vol. 2, pg. 185,213-214,222.

73   Robert Service (whom we met in the Syndrome One), op. cit. pg. 63. Written in Paris in May 1914. He did succeed quite well as a writer of popular verse; but he never gained the rank of a true poet.

there are equally pleasures the poor alone experience. If there is a sorrow in poverty, there is also a sorrow in riches. If much is given to some, from them also much is required (Lu 12:48). No one has ever spoken with greater wisdom than the man who said -

> *"Give me neither poverty nor riches, but just the food I need each day. For if you give me too much, I might turn my back on you, saying, 'Who is God anyway?' And if you give me too little, I might be tempted to grab what is not mine, and so dishonour the name of my God" (Pr 30:8,9).*

Preachers are just as much obligated to echo that wisdom as are the members of their congregations. It does not mean that you should reject high success, or great wealth, if they lie in God's purpose for you; but do not lust after them. Accept without complaint the orderings of providence. Let the Father's will be done!

Perils On The Heights

> *"Uneasy lies the head that wears a crown" wrote Shakespeare, [74] and that can be as true in church life as anywhere else. The higher you are, the further there is to fall; the more you have, the more there is to lose; the loftier your renown, the deeper may be your disgrace. Thus Seneca wrote -*
> *No state of life endures; pleasure and pain*
> *Take each their turn; and pleasure's turn is shorter.*
> *Time swiftly changes highest into lowest.*
> *That king - who can give crowns away;*
> *Before whose feet nations have bowed*
> *In fearful homage . . .*
> *Fears for his crown,*
> *Anxiously scans the signs of Fate,*
> *Dreads treacherous Time and the swift chance*

---

74   Henry IV, Part Two, III,i,31.

That can make all things change . . . [75]

Such sentiments were often expressed by Seneca in his various writings, and they are well summarised in the words sung by the Chorus near the end of his play, Octavia -

> *Happy lies poverty, content, unseen*
> *Under her humble roof.*
> *The high house shakes*
> *More often to the winds of heaven*
> *Or falls to Fortune's stroke.* [76]

And somewhere else in his writings he says that "a great fortune is a great slavery." [77]

None of that, of course, is an excuse for cowardice or sloth, or for failing to achieve all that God has given you to achieve; but it does say that you have no cause either to envy the highly successful or to be discontent with whatever level of accomplishment does lie within your grasp.

Choices To Make

Since they cannot reasonably hope to build or lead a large church, average pastors have five options -

Be content with an average church, which in Australia (among Pentecostals) is currently a congregation of about 100. [78] Any shepherd who truly loves and cares for a flock of a hundred of God's sheep will find more than enough joyful work to occupy a lifetime and bring a sweet reward in the kingdom.

---

75   Op. cit. pg. 71-72.

76   Ibid. pg. 293.

77   He spoke from experience, for he amassed an enormous fortune, and then lost it all!

78   The average for all Protestant/Pentecostal congregations is below 50 at church on Sunday morning.

Take a more limited role in the church; that is, learn the art of delegation, which means yielding authority over various areas of ministry to others who are more skilled. Thus the "one-talent" man (already mentioned above) could have fulfilled his lord's expectations simply by calling on the expertise of the money-lenders (Mt 25:24-27). However, many people do find delegation emotionally and temperamentally impossible. [79] In their heads they know what to do, but their hearts prevent them! there is no point saying to them "Delegate! Delegate!" for they simply cannot do it. For them it is like asking a devoted mother to delegate the nurture and upbringing of her infant to a stranger. Nothing will persuade her to hand the child over! Such leaders must either go back to the first choice, and content themselves with what they have, or consider one of the three choices that follow.

Accept a subordinate role, either in their own church or as a staff member in a larger church. Sometimes the best action a pastor can take to promote local church growth is simply to remove himself or herself from leadership. Having taken the church as far as he can, perhaps it is now time for him to invite a more gifted leader to take his place? There are also capable people who do not function well as senior pastors of a church, but will flourish as a member of the ministry team of a larger congregation.

Step out of the ministry, for they may have mistakenly read a call to lay service as a full-time call. Or perhaps they should move to another church in another city or suburb. Among the syndromes discussed in this book I could have added The "Dusty Shoe" Syndrome - that is, servants of Christ who refuse to heed the Master's advice and "shake off the dust of that place from your feet" (Lu 10:11). A pastor may fail in one place, yet reap a great harvest in another.

---

79 Note that delegation by itself is not enough; there must also be leadership. Leaders should delegate, not to be released from leadership, but so that attention can be given to the broader vision, and to motivating and disciplining the members of the staff. Many pastors delegate falsely, only so that they can be free to pursue their own interests.

No one, however, can succeed anywhere until the fear of failure has been overcome. If you don't know how to fail, neither will you learn how to succeed. After helping his team to win three national basketball titles, the USA champion Michael Jordan decided to shift from basketball to baseball. When friends and advisers remonstrated with him he replied, "I am not afraid to fail!" He was not, of course, referring to failure as a human being, but only to failure in one area of professional achievement. Pastors, too, must overcome the fear of failure, and if their ministry is not working be willing to consider a change of place, or even of call.

Repeat what he or she has already done, which for most will be the best alternative. Have you gathered together a congregation of fifty, and then plateaued? Well, launch out from that base to the next town or suburb and do it again! Instead of saying, "I have proved that I will never build a congregation of a hundred," say rather, "I have proved that I can build a congregation of fifty!" And go and do it again, and again. You may soon find that instead of one congregation of fifty you will have four or five, and be ministering in fact to a couple of hundred people!

Obedience Is Better Than Sacrifice

Let me repeat here this important principle: none of us should attempt more than God has called us to do, but neither may we dare to do less! The Father does not want sacrifice so much as obedience - yet that is perhaps the hardest thing of all for us to accept!

> *"True is it that, in these days, man can do almost all things, only not obey. True likewise that whoso cannot obey, cannot be free, still less bear rule; he that is the inferior of nothing, can be the superior of nothing, the equal of nothing."* [80]

---

80   Thomas Carlyle, op. cit., Book Three, Chapter Seven.

Chapter Ten

THE "WRONG FOCUS" SYNDROME

A Christian's eye ought not to be fixed on this world, but only on what the end of the day will show -

> *"The hero then will know how to wait, as well as to make haste. All good abides with him who waiteth wisely; we shall sooner overtake the dawn by remaining here than by hurrying over the hills to the west. Be assured that every man's success is in proportion to his average ability. The meadow flowers spring and bloom where the waters annually deposit their slime, not where they reach in some freshet only. A man is not his hope, nor his despair, nor yet his past deed. We know not yet what we have done, still less what we are doing. Wait till evening, and other parts of our day's work will shine than we had thought at noon, and we shall discover the real purport of our toil. As when the farmer has reached the end of the furrow and looks back, he can tell best where the pressed earth shines most."* [81]

---

81   Thoreau, op. cit. pg. 104.   Thoreau was himself an example of his philosophy. He turned his back on a fortune and chose instead to live in humble circumstances so that he could better pursue his writing goals. His first book, the one quoted from above, although it is now much admired, was a failure in his lifetime. Out of a print run of 1000 copies, 706 were returned to him by the publisher. Thoreau noted in his journal: "I now have a library of nearly nine hundred volumes, over seven hundred of which I wrote myself." His most famous work is Walden (1854), which is recognised as an American classic.

Read again the text that stands at the beginning of the previous chapter. Did you notice how little of Paul's ministerial recommendation consisted of achievement, and how much is focussed on character? Who you are is vastly more important to God than what you have done. You have full control over who you are; you can influence only slightly what you do. That is because so much of what you do rests upon factors you cannot control - that is, who you are, where you were born, where you live, how you were raised, what opportunities come your way, and the like.

For example, suppose we take a group of average pastors in Australia and measure the level of statistical success they experience. We then go to a land where the church is enjoying explosive growth, gather a similar group of pastors in that land, and measure how well they are doing. You will no doubt find that the second group seems highly successful, while the first is struggling. Will you now say that the Australian pastors must be deficient in faith, zeal, prayer, and skill? That would be absurd. Indeed, take the two groups and oblige them to change countries, and you will now find that those who were once successful are now struggling, while those who were struggling are now successful! In other words, achieving vigorous church growth depends at least as much upon outward circumstances as it does upon spiritual dynamics.

So there is seldom any valid reason to suppose that one group of Spirit-filled pastors is less capable or spiritual than another. The difference in the results achieved by each group is related mostly to "time and chance" (Ec 9:11-12). For that reason, the worst of men have sometimes conquered the earth; the best of men have sometimes failed to make any mark. Hence the things that Paul felt are a pastor's chief crown are -

➢ providing an example of CONDUCT

• "we recommend ourselves to you by our pure behaviour"

- holding to a true CONFESSION

  - "we recommend ourselves to you by our sound doctrine"

- showing a gracious CHARACTER

  - "we recommend ourselves to you by our patience and kindness"

- endowed with the CHARISMATA

  - "we recommend ourselves to you by the gifts of the Holy Spirit"

- overflowing with real CONCERN

  - "we recommend ourselves to you by our genuine love"

- strongly and boldly CATECHISING

  - "we recommend ourselves to you by proclamation of the truth"

- divinely CALLED and CAPABLE

  - "we recommend ourselves to you by the power of God"

Only in the last item does Paul begin to think in the familiar modern terms of "power". Even then he follows it in the next breath with a parade of suffering, misery, and hardship endured for the kingdom! (vs. 8-10; 11:23-28). In the end, it is not fame that counts, but name, which is a principle that noble thinkers have always known -

> *"All things fade into the storied past, and in a little while are shrouded in oblivion. Even to men whose lives were a blaze of glory this comes to pass; as for the rest, the breath is hardly out of them before, in Homer's words, they are 'lost to sight alike and hearsay'. What, after all, is immortal fame? An empty, hollow thing. To what, then, must we aspire? This, and this alone: the just thought, the*

unselfish act, the tongue that offers no falsehood, the temper that greets each passing event as something predestined, expected, and emanating from the One source and origin." [82]

Did Jesus not mean it when he said that the world will "know that we are his disciples when they see that we love one another"? Only in this can we surpass the world, which in matters of multitudes and wealth will always far surpass the church! The best of minds have always reckoned love to be the only goal finally worth attaining. Once two young lovers met among the ruins of a long-decayed castle. A poet saw them there, and measured their love against the ancient kingdom, with its forgotten splendour, its banished might, its decayed riches, and he came to an inescapable conclusion -

Oh, heart! oh, blood that freezes, blood that burns!
Earth's returns
For whole centuries of folly, noise, and sin!
Shut them in
With their triumphs, and their glories, and the rest.
Love is best! [83]

Therefore be warned against the perils that are today besetting many parts of the Pentecostal movement:

Once separated from the world, now eager to reflect its lifestyle, to chase after its material goals, to ape its concept of "success". But we are called to pursue, not happiness, but holiness (He 12:14).

Once scorned the yoke of legalism, now devising new sets of rules and regulations about going, doing, eating, wearing, and behaving. But the kingdom of God does not consist of such rules, but of righteousness, peace, and joy in the Holy Spirit (Ro 14:17; Cl 2:16-23).

---

82   The Emperor Marcus Aurelius, op. cit. Book Four, #33; pg. 71.

83   Robert Browning, Love Among the Ruins; final lines.

Once opposed to fixed creeds, now busy setting up and defending the infallibility of their own dogmas, the unyielding correctness of their own cultural mores, the absolute truth of their own social taboos. But while each church must be committed to sound doctrine, let us avoid the conceit of claiming that our group alone possesses perfect truth, free of any error.

Once embraced miracles as the sign of a new era, now use them as crowd-catching gimmicks. But "falling under the power", "holy laughter", etc, were not the kind of miracles the apostles used to turn their world upside-down. They depended rather upon true healings, deliverances, and genuine acts of power

Once rejoiced in personal liberty and church autonomy, now building ever-bigger bureaucracies. The sodality of the early church, which functioned as a living fellowship, a loving brotherhood, an open association, has been changed into the modality of the modern church, with its closed corporate structure, its hierarchies, its stifling conformities.

Once majored on sound doctrine, now focussed on the pursuit of personal happiness, statistical success, and organisational growth. But we dare not tolerate intolerable deviations from truth just to catch a crowd.

Once saw worship as a sacrifice to offer, now a sensation to be experienced, so that in many places it has become shallow, undemanding, a noisy revelry, rather than a dedicated offering of one's whole life to God. But we dare not accept any form of worship that is not an expression of total surrender to the lordship of Christ, and a demonstration of a life lived in full conformity to his will.

Once focussed externally on evangelism, now internally on structure and conformity, and on buildings, programmes, and organisation. But what use is pride in our ever-finer buildings, and our ever-growing wealth, if it reflects a luke-warm Christianity that provokes no opposition from the world, nor shows any real separation from it?

Once content with Holy Spirit baptism, now restlessly craving some new stimulant; But if people were truly baptised in the Spirit, and learning how to live and walk in the Spirit, they would not be always itching for some new "key" to victorious life in Christ

Once built around prayer and Pentecostal evangelism, now depending on programmes, promotions, and entertainment.

Instead of a cry to maintain biblical standards there is a general push toward pastors who are friendly, sympathetic, faulty, ambivalent, one of us, rather than self-controlled, courageous, imaginative, assured, strong. Sadly, many congregations do prefer a shepherd who maintains the status quo, rather than a leader who forces them, under the absolute lordship of Christ, to break into new dimensions of faith, growth, discipleship, and the genuinely supernatural.

Our goal should be that the faith of the people "might not rest upon human wisdom, but upon the power of God" (1 Co 2:5); instead it is often now the very people of God who insist that their pastor (against the teaching of Paul, 1 Co 2:1-4) should dangle in front of them "eloquent" sermons, and "clever" programmes, and an enticing "vision" in place of the Cross of Christ. They are not attracted to a crucified life, they do not really want the power of God, but prefer exciting programmes and mere sensation instead.

You should not pander to such fleshy demands, but set yourself to obey only the Lord Christ.

Chapter Eleven

THE "FOOLISH HUNTER" SYNDROME

"Avoid as you would the plague a clergyman who is also a man of business." [84]

A pastor in western Wisconsin once asked me how he could revitalise his church. I suggested three things that surprised him (he was hoping for some magical techniques):

➢ disciple a group of leaders

➢ bathe his ministry in prayer

➢ reach out for miracles.

That seems to me to be the biblical method; but many have instead replaced charismatic power with clever programmes. Consequently I have seen quite small churches dissipating their energies through a dozen or more departments. No doubt programmes and projects have their place, but there are two things to watch -

YOUR VISION

Each local church should be kept homogeneous, focussed on one prime goal, for you cannot pursue contrary goals. Too much diversification has proved ruinous to many previously successful enterprises.

Even more destructive is an attempt to embrace goals that prove to be mutually exclusive. Temper your zeal for complexity. Resist the urge to multiply departments. You don't have to do everything that can be done by a church, only what is right for your church to

---

84   Jerome (circa 342-420); Letters #52.

do. Be like a hunter, who knows he cannot chase the entire herd, but must focus upon one prey -

> *"My child, do not take on too many projects; if you try to do too much you will simply bring yourself to grief. No matter how hard you run, you will not catch up; and if you try to escape, your burdens will chase you relentlessly.*
>
> *"Some people frantically toil and struggle, only to fall ever further behind, while others are slow, always needing help, and stay weak and poor. Yet the Lord may look upon them pleasantly, lift them out of their sorry plight, and to everyone's amazement raise them to high honour!*
>
> *"In the end, good fortune and bad, life and death, poverty and riches, all come from the hand of the Lord" (Sir 11:10-14).*
>
> *"This leads us back again to the impossibility of the pastoral role, given current expectations of clergy by laity and church executives. It is no secret that of all occupations parish clergy have among the highest incidences of physical and emotional breakdowns. . . .*
>
> *"(Here is) a statistic that should be of no surprise to us: The one profession that tops all other professions in this country (the USA) for incidence of heart attacks, strokes, cancer, diabetes, and alcoholism is the Jewish Rabbi. . . . (Research) indicates that one in every five clergy is severely burned out. A key contributing factor is the expectation that clergy be competent in all areas of ministry. It isn't scriptural or even reasonable, yet the expectation continues."* [85]

---

85   Personality Type and Religious Leadership, by Roy M. Oswald and Otto Kroeger; Alban Institute, New York, 1988; pg. 37-38.

Unhappily, pastors themselves often create these ridiculous expectations. They act as if they were the possessors of all wisdom, able to do all the work of the ministry well, skilled in solving every problem, qualified to meet every need, equal to every demand. Such inexcusable hubris must seem preposterous to God, like the strutting arrogance of the pompous Emperor of Lilliput -

> *"GOLBASTO MOMAREN EVLAME GURDILO SHEFIN MULLY ULLY GUE, Most Might Emperor of Lilliput, Delight and terror of the Universe, whose dominions extend five Thousand Blustrugs, (about twelve miles in Circumference) to the extremities of the Globe: Monarch of all Monarchs: Taller than the Sons of Men; whose Feet press down to the Centre, and whose Head strikes against the Sun: At whose Nod the Princes of the Earth shake their Knees; pleasant as the Spring, comfortable as the Summer, fruitful as Autumn, dreadful as Winter. His most sublime Majesty proposeth to the Man-Mountain, lately arrived at our Celestial Dominions, the following Articles, which by a solemn Oath he shall be obliged to perform . . . (then follow the Articles) . . . "*[86]

A little more willingness to admit ignorance and inability would save many a pastor from collapse.

YOUR PRIORITIES

Any church eager to follow the New Testament model must be committed to a ministry attended by signs, wonders, and miracles

---

[86] Gulliver's Travels, by Jonathan Swift (1667-1745); Oxford University Press, New York, 1977; pg. 29,30. The emperor promised to give Gulliver his freedom providing the Englishman agreed to a certain set of conditions. The emperor's proclamation of pardon and liberty began with the words quoted above.

(Mk 16:20; Ac 2:43; 5:12-16; Ro 15:18-19; 1 Co 2:4-5; 1 Th 1:4-5; He 2:4). The kingdom of darkness is a supernatural kingdom and nothing less than a supernatural church can hope to overthrow it. A church that depends primarily upon advertising, activities, associations, administrations for its life and growth may achieve great statistical success, but it will pose little real threat to the devil. After all, Jesus did not say, "Go into all the world and gather a crowd!" (which the world can do better than we can anyway), but "Go into all the world and make disciples!"

No doubt we should use every tool and resource available to us to help us to fulfil the task of the evangel, but they must always be subsidiary to "a demonstration of the power of the Spirit" (1 Co 2:4).

However, don't believe every "miracle" that comes along; ascribe a divine origin only to what is endorsed in scripture. Despite the superior attitude we are prone to adopt toward the gullible people of the middle ages, or toward simple people of other cultures in our own time, superstition is rampant also among western Pentecostals. Nothing has changed except the nature of the "miracles" that leave the unwary gaping. In the past the credulous were impressed by the stigmata, levitations, sobbings, apparitions of the Virgin, and the like. [87] Now we are prone to be over-awed by various forms of religious catalepsy, prostrations, laughter, and other such phenomena - although they too were part of the mediaeval religious world, and have often occurred over the centuries in both Christian and pagan settings. You should recognise that such phenomena are largely conditioned by

---

87   Such phenomena have been part of the religious experience of mystics in all branches of the church, and also in the great non-Christian religions. For example, one of the greatest of the English Roman Catholic mystics was the illiterate, but very intelligent, Margery Kempe (c. 1373-c. 1440). Her experiences are described in her autobiography (which she dictated), The Book Of Margery Kempe. In it she talks about falling into compulsive weepings, howlings, shoutings, laughings, and the like. You will find a passage from it quoted in Part Two - Chapter One, below.

(1) Cultural Factors

For example, the "stigmata" are seldom seen now. They do not appeal to modern western audiences, who would probably be horrified rather than impressed by dripping blood. So a phenomenon that was greatly renowned in the past, and is still renowned in some parts of the world, is most unlikely to be promoted in any western Pentecostal church. So out of the vast array of possible religious or spiritual phenomena [88] only those that are socially acceptable are likely to occur in any one place.

(2) Changing Definitions

For example, until recently, "prostration" during evangelical revivals signified a sense of guilt, deep conviction of sin, and tearful repentance. Thus Spurgeon wrote (Treasury of David, on Ps 6:6-7) -

> *"May not this explain some of the convulsions and hysterical attacks which have been experienced under convictions in the revivals in Ireland? Is it surprising that some should be smitten to the earth, and begin to cry aloud, when we find that David himself made his bed to swim, and grew old while he was under the heavy hand of God?"*

As I have already suggested, the differences between those earlier prostrations and some modern versions of the same experience probably arise from cultural and/or environmental conditioning, from peer group examples, and the like. On the whole, crowds will behave as they have been taught to behave, whether consciously or unconsciously, and the psychological pressure can

---

88 Paul calls them *"pneumatika"*, and hopes that Christians will not remain ignorant about them, but will learn how to distinguish between those that are truly the work of the Holy Spirit, those that are demonic, and those that are simply a common part of human religious experience (1 Co 12:1 ff.)

become almost irresistible, both upon those who have had no previous knowledge of the phenomenon and upon those who try to resist it.

Nowadays the idea of collapsing under awful conviction of sin rests uncomfortably with our comfort-loving congregations! So we have re-defined prostration to mean "falling under the power", and given it the more exciting and appealing character of a divinely wrought act of joyous blessing!

I do not mean that such phenomena are wrong, or even undesirable, just that we ought to be mature enough to recognise how deeply they depend upon cultural environment, community expectations, and changing expectations of what God should do among his people. If they serve a useful purpose, if they bring grace into the lives of the people, if they glorify Christ and help to build the church, then they may be allowed, if not encouraged. But let us keep our attention where it should be, on Christ and the Cross, not on some passing religious fad, some shifting wind of spiritual experience.

Chapter Twelve

THE "DOUBLE PORTION" SYNDROME

Many modern preachers have cried out to God for a repetition of Elisha's "double portion" in their lives (2 Kg 2:9). And indeed, Elisha's prayer was remarkably answered, for it has often been noticed that while Elijah wrought seven miracles, Elisha performed just twice as many, fourteen!

However, before rushing off to claim the same for yourself, note -

1. No later prophet either asked or expected to emulate Elisha. They were all content to function within the parameters of the prophetic call each one received from God (how different, for example, is the style of Ezekiel to that, say, of Isaiah).

2. We have received from God a much higher and greater gift than a mere "double portion"! Paul characterised our state as "constantly advancing from glory to glory!" Our problem is not that we lack anything we need to fulfil splendidly our missionary mandate, but that we do not employ what the Lord has already given us! [89]

CONCLUSION

During the second century the Roman Empire was governed by an extraordinary succession of fine monarchs (Nerva, Trajan, Hadrian, Antoninus, Marcus Aurelius). Under their wise rule the 200 million inhabitants of the empire enjoyed a level of peace, happiness, and prosperity beyond anything the ancient world had ever known. The last of them, Marcus Aurelius, was the adopted

---

89   This paragraph nicely summarises the main thrust of the second part of this book, "Models of Revival".

son of Antoninus, to whom Marcus gave perhaps the noblest character that ever one man has ascribed to another.[90].

Neither of the emperors had any knowledge of the true God, yet they displayed a quality of nobility, of graciousness, of adherence to duty, that any servant of Christ would surely be happy to attain. Here then is the admonition Marcus wrote to himself to follow the example of his royal predecessor -

> *"Be in all things Antoninus' disciple; remember his insistence on the control of conduct by reason; his calm composure on all occasions, and his own holiness; the serenity of his look and the sweetness of his manner; his scorn of notoriety, and his zeal for the mastery of the facts; how he would never dismiss a subject until he had looked thoroughly into it and understood it clearly; how he would suffer unjust criticism without replying in kind; how he was never hasty, and no friend to tale-bearers; shrewd in his judgments of men and manners, yet never censorious; wholly free from nervousness, suspicion, and over-subtlety; how easily satisfied he was in such matters as lodging, bed, dress, meals, and service; how industrious, and how patient; how, thanks to his frugal diet, he could remain at work from morning till night . . .; how firm and constant he was in friendship, tolerating the most outspoken opposition to his own opinions, and welcoming any suggested amendments; what reverence, untainted by the smallest trace of superstition, he showed to the gods. Remember all*

---

90   Some commentators think that the man portrayed by Marcus may unconsciously more resemble the son than his adoptive father.

this, so that when your own last hour comes your conscience may be as clear as his!" [91]

---

91 Maxwell Staniforth, op. cit. Book 6, #30. The emperor did in fact die quickly and peacefully in his tent, after contracting a fever while leading his army in a battle against invaders. He was 60 years old, and had reigned 20 years, most of them spent in warfare defending the Roman frontiers.

Part Two

MODELS OF REVIVAL

Chapter Thirteen

SPIRITUAL AWAKENING

INTRODUCTION

There are two common approaches to the theme of "revival" among evangelical Christians, and also, unfortunately, among many charismatics. I say "unfortunately" because neither of these approaches reflects the New Testament model. This study will argue for a third approach (see Chapter Three below), which, it will be claimed, does conform to the New Testament pattern.

The subject is an important one, because one's assumptions concerning "revival" have a determinative effect upon many other areas of personal and corporate life in the local church. Your views on revival will shape your -

approach to prayer

➢ where revival is defined as an unpredictable divine visitation then prayer will be focussed on fervent pleading for God to act; but where revival is seen as a product of fulfilling the Great Commission then prayer will be focussed on the Lord prospering the evangel.

expectations from God

➢ one view leads to a fatalistic crying out to the Lord for showers of mercy; the other leads to a bold seizure of all the resources that are available in Christ, thus ensuring that his missionary mandate is fulfilled (Mt 28:19-20; Mk 16:15-20).

ministry goals

➤ where revival is seen as a more or less arbitrary act by God, ministry tends to be focussed on patiently keeping the church together until God chooses to send a "revival"; but where revival is measured by successful evangelism and church planting, then ministry tends to be focussed upon confident outreach, with an expectation of continuous life and blessing.

attitudes towards yourself

➤ the first view tends to create constant introspection, based upon a belief that "revival" cannot happen until the church becomes "holy"; the other leads to an acceptance of righteousness in Christ, and to confidence that God will use the church as it is.

concepts of the church

➤ the first view is prone to see the church as weak, helpless, and unable to fulfil the demands of the evangel unless a "revival" first happens; the other sees the church, with all its faults, as fully competent to rise up in Jesus' name and reap the waiting harvest.

concepts of the world

➤ the first view tends toward a ghetto complex, where the church is huddled together against the world, which it sees only in terms of enmity and corruption; the other looks upon the world more positively, with strong confidence that brave preaching of the gospel will attract a fruitful response.

ideas on church polity

> the principles upon which the local church is based, its organisational dynamics, its style and emphases, its expectations and attitudes, will all be deeply influenced (whether consciously or unconsciously) by its philosophy of revival.

There is, then, hardly any area of personal or congregational life that remains unaffected by the concept of revival held by the local church. Which view should we adopt? I make no claim to infallibility, nor to final authority; but you will at least find here some ideas that deserve to be carefully considered .

Let me begin with the first of the two common models of revival, one that is widely held among evangelical, charismatic, and Pentecostal Christians. We could call it

THE SPIRITUAL AWAKENING MODEL

In each of the three Models presented here I will follow this structure:

> a definition of the model

> a description of the model

> the assumptions upon which the model is based

> objections against the model (for the first two models only)

> and then (for the third model only) an application of the model.

Accordingly, our study of the "spiritual awakening model" begins with a

DEFINITION

In the "spiritual awakening" model "revival" is defined as a powerful and mostly sovereign work of God - a hurricane of the Holy Spirit that sweeps across a local community, or perhaps a whole state, and leads to rapid growth in the church. Such heavenly visitations, it is said, are mostly determined by will and actions of God, yet they can be promoted by fervent and continuous prayer and fasting. However, the time, manner, and place, of the visitation cannot be known beforehand; so the church must wait patiently for God to respond to the pleas of his people. That response may come swiftly, or may be delayed for decades, or may not come at all; for "revival" is seen as an altogether sovereign act of God, who may send it or not as he pleases.

DESCRIPTION

When and if such "revivals" occur, they have certain common factors -

They tend to be centred on groups that adhere to a certain kind of subjective piety, and are ignored or rejected by most people. The reason is simple. The intense religious and/or spiritual experiences that are commonly part of such "visitations" are unappealing to large segments of society. For the same reason, they seldom touch established denominations, which does not always mean that those denominations are backslidden. In fact the lack of response by many groups and/or congregations to the "revival" may indicate nothing more than a preference for a calmer manner of relating to the gospel and to God. It is not necessarily God, or even the work of God, that they are rejecting, but rather the behaviour of those who are enjoying the "revival". (Of course, there are people or groups who scorn "revivals", or any unusual work of the Spirit, just because they do lack any hunger for God and reject any possibility of a supernatural visitation.)

"Revivals" usually bring a rapid and massive, but often short-term, ingathering of souls. They tend to have a short life because the energy of the "revival" may be dissipated by lack of restraint. The saints become worn-out from attending too many meetings, exhausted by the inordinate length of the meetings, and drained emotionally by staying on a spiritual "high" for an extended period. People cannot maintain a high level of intense fervour for prolonged weeks and months.

"Revivals" are often accompanied by ardent behaviour, which may be a source of as much harm as it is of much good - for impassioned actions attract some people and repel others. Some of the phenomena often observed in such "awakenings" are public confession of sin, loud outcries, tears, convulsions, prostrations, uninhibited or uncontrollable laughter, and the like. John Wesley, for example, first encouraged, but later discouraged such phenomena in his meetings. He realised that while they helped initially to attract the crowds and to give notoriety to his meetings, their long-term result was more negative than positive. He eventually took vigorous steps to eliminate them, even to the extent (so I have read somewhere) of having buckets of water thrown over people who fell into any kind of cataleptic behaviour! [92]

Such phenomena, of course, are by no means limited to Pentecostals; they are part of the religious experience of mystics in all branches of the church, and also in the great non-Christian religions. For example, one of the greatest of the English Roman

---

[92] There is further comment on these matters in my book "Equipped to Serve", and also in the lecture notes associated with it. The two following passages are also taken from the same sources, and from the study "The Glories of Glossolalia - Part Two".

Catholic mystics was the illiterate, but very intelligent, Margery Kempe (c. 1373-c. 1440). Her experiences are described in her autobiography (which she dictated). In it she talks about falling into compulsive weepings, howlings, shoutings, laughings, and the like. Here is one of many similar passages -

> *"She told him (her amanuensis) how sometimes the Father of Heaven conversed with her soul as plainly and as certainly as one friend speaks to another through bodily speech. Sometimes the Second Person in the Trinity, sometimes all Three Persons in Trinity and one substance in Godhead, spoke to her soul, and informed her in her faith and in his love - how she should love him, worship him, and dread him. . . . Sometimes our Lady spoke to her mind; sometimes St Peter, sometimes St Paul, sometimes St Katherine, or whatever saint in heaven she was devoted to, appeared to her soul and taught her how she should love our Lord, and how she should please him. These conversations were so sweet, so holy and so devout, that often this creature could not bear it, but fell down and twisted and wrenched her body about, and made remarkable faces and gestures, with vehement sobbings and great abundance of tears, sometimes saying 'Jesus, mercy,' and sometimes, 'I die.'"* [93]

Did those experiences come from God? Were they altogether acts of the Holy Spirit? If so, why were apparitions of Mary and the Apostles added to those of Christ? I do not doubt (after reading her book) that Margery Kempe was a woman of deep devotion, sound theology (within the Roman Catholic tradition), and abounding love for Christ. So I cannot denounce her prostrations as demonic; but neither can I attribute them solely to God. Plainly,

---

93 The Book of Margery Kempe, tr. by B. A. Windeatt; Penguin Books, 1988; pg. 75.

her experiences were a mixture of the divine with the human, and all of it shaped by the religious and cultural milieu in which she lived and worshipped.

I have already mentioned this, but it will probably bear repetition, that religious prostrations, and other such seizures, were formerly associated by both evangelical and Pentecostal Christians, not with blessing (as they tend to be in modern Pentecostal circles), but with deep conviction of sin! I have read several accounts of past revivals, in which excited comment was made on the sight of people falling down, groaning and sobbing because of the wrenching guilt they were suffering. The main reason for our modern change in focus seems to be cultural rather than spiritual. We today prefer feelings of joy to those of guilt! Visions of hell are no longer appropriate; we favour lovely vistas of heaven. I do not mean that the phenomena that are often associated with "revivals" are false, or that God does not make use of them; I mean only that we must admit the inescapable part played in them by personal and social influences.

ASSUMPTIONS

Around the world, millions of Christians are praying for "revival". Why? Underlying their fervent pleas there is a major, and in my opinion an ultimately devastating, assumption: without such a "revival" the church is condemned to labour with small success.

That leads to a second assumption: the prime task of evangelical Christians is to pray unceasingly for "revival", so that the church may effectively fulfil its mission.

As a consequence of those two assumptions, "histories of revival" often devote much attention to tracking down the person(s) whose prayers are assumed to have been the match that kindled the fires of heaven. Their intercessions carved a tunnel through which the Holy Spirit blew like a gale upon the earth. However, on the idea of prayer as the main cause of spiritual awakenings, I will risk the ire of a host of devout people by offering the following suggestions-

No-one could sensibly deny that prayer has an important part to play in the success of Christian ministry, nor should anyone wish to stop prayer. By all means let us ask the Lord to open the windows of heaven and pour out more blessing than the land can contain! [94] What true Christian would do other than rejoice if the Lord should visit the nation and grant the churches an incredible harvest of souls?

Nonetheless, I cannot forget all those passionate, long-continuing prayer meetings that have not resulted in a "revival" - many of which I have attended myself across some 42 years of ministry. Millions of people have spent hundreds of hours in prayer throughout their lifetime, crying for revival, yet have died without seeing a visitation of God.

Indeed on a purely statistical basis the evidence is strongly against prayer having much to do with a divine visitation!

The overwhelming evidence of church history is that prayer (by itself) is largely ineffective in producing a revival[95].

---

94 Note, however, the original setting of the "windows of heaven" idea. It comes from Malachi, who attributes it, not to prayer, but to faithful tithing! (3:10-12) Why? No doubt because when the Lord prospers them, then the servants of God will have more than enough resources to do all that God has commanded. They will be able to propagate the law of the Lord to the ends of the earth. The people of God, the farmers, workers, governors, etc, who give faithfully, will also find the work of their hands prospered by the Lord so remarkably, that all will have to acknowledge them as blessed by God! At least that is how the promise was intended to work under the old covenant. It operates a little differently now, but the underlying principle is much the same.

95 That is, match the countless thousands of prayer meetings (many of which were sustained across several decades) that have not produced a revival against the tiny handful that do appear to have stirred a spiritual awakening.

Prayer, of course, has a vital part to play in bringing the saints to spiritual maturity and in keeping the local church alive in godliness. Perhaps more importantly, it also has astonishing power to influence the social environment, helping to create the circumstances in which the church can best fulfil its missionary mandate - see 1 Timothy 2:1-3. There (as I have already mentioned) Paul takes it for granted that prayer can change government policy, thus creating an environment in which the church can peaceably pursue its mission. Without quietness and peace the church cannot effectively preach Christ nor plant new congregations. Note again how Paul sees prayer more as helping the church to fulfil its missionary mandate than as a trigger for a divine visitation. Apparently prayer alone cannot ordinarily change the hearts and minds of the millions outside the church, nor dispose them to yield to the claims of Christ. Only when the wider environment is conducive to a spiritual awakening is prayer likely to be a significant factor in promoting a revival.

We may say then that prayer undoubtedly helps a revival along but is not by itself the usual cause of a far-reaching visitation by God. Think about the thousands of Pentecostals from one end of Australia to the other who for decades have prayed most earnestly for a revival. Yet after nearly a century of ministry, we Pentecostals still number barely 1.5% of the population, and we seem as far away from seeing a nation-wide "revival" as ever our now-dead Pentecostal forefathers were. Did they not pray fervently enough? Are our prayers also sadly deficient? I doubt it. Many of them prayed as heartily, as persistently, as fiercely, as any of those in the past whose prayers the historians have said were the seed of a great "revival". [96]

---

96   Note also: (despite the fervent prayers of those thousands of saints) church attendance in Australia has remained fairly stable since colonial times, at between 20-30% of the population. At the time of writing these notes (1994), some 45% attend church occasionally, and 24% regularly (that is, more than once a month), and 70% call themselves Christians. There are also encouraging indications that the decline in church attendance

Should we then stop praying? Of course not! But how should we pray? The answer to that question will be taken up when we look at the third "model" of revival, below.

OBJECTIONS

LESSONS FROM HISTORY

There is much that is highly commendable in the "spiritual awakening" model of revival. Who among us would not be glad beyond measure if our nation were shaken by a mighty "revival", leading to packed churches, righteous legislation, the crushing of iniquity, and the exalting of holiness throughout the land? May the Lord indeed do such a glorious and gracious work across our nation! For such a visitation by God we should certainly pray from time to time, in real hope that the Lord will be gracious to us, hear our cry, and sweep from coast to coast in a hurricane of blessing!

Nonetheless, there are a number of factors that make the "spiritual awakening model" unsuitable as a major [97] focus of Christian thinking and praying. Therefore, in contrast with all that has been written over the years in its favour, let me suggest that -

It does not conform either to the teaching or example of the early church.

There is simply no biblical warrant for the common evangelical concept of "revival". The word is not found in the New Testament, it does not reflect apostolic concepts, nor is any early prayer focussed upon it. On the contrary, the apostles emphasised only

---

characteristic of the past few years has been arrested, and that most, if not all denominations, are either stable in their attendance or beginning to increase again.

97   Please note the emphasis. I am not altogether rejecting the model, but simply decrying what seems to me to be an undeserved emphasis upon it.

Pentecostal evangelism and church planting (see Part Three below).

The mere fact that such "revivals" have occurred in history does not establish them as the ideal model to follow.

God is often obliged to accommodate his actions to faulty understanding and expectations among his people. Our aim should be to conform, not to church history, but to the clearly defined New Testament paradigm. There are, of course, many aspects of the government and structure of the early church that remain uncertain; but on this matter at least there can be no dispute: they "turned the world upside down" simply by preaching Christ in the power of the Holy Spirit. What better example can there be for us to follow?

History shows that "revivals" are not solely the result of some mysterious decision by God in response to the fervent prayers of the saints.

Consider the following -

A. Revivals are not wholly supernatural effusions, given in answer to fervent intercession by the church, for if they were, they would surely occur much more frequently. How many thousands (indeed millions) of Christians have cried out to God year after year for revival, yet in vain. Decades, and generations, have passed by, and the longed-for revival has not come. Why? Simply this: widespread spiritual awakenings seldom occur, because they cannot be divorced from social, cultural, political, and situational influences.

Illustration: take an immensely successful pastor away from his huge church and locate him in another land. Will he automatically achieve the same level of "success" from the same amount of toil, prayer, and faith? Perhaps. But he is just as likely to experience scant result; indeed, violent persecution may instead be the major harvest reaped! The very spiritual energy that brought him honour and renown in one environment may in another bring him imprisonment or death. Has he then failed? Has God gone away from his ministry? Of course not. Nothing has changed except the situation in which he is ministering - but that changes everything!

B. Note also: in times of revival, all religions tend to flourish (not just the church). Why? Because social conditions that cause an awakening of spiritual hunger, and that are congenial to preaching the gospel, are just as favourable for other major faiths. In such conditions, especially in a multicultural society, temple, mosque, synagogue, and church are all likely to flourish together. If Christians happen to get there first, then the Christians will enjoy what they are pleased to call a "revival"; but if (say) Buddhists or Muslims are the first to take advantage of the opportunity, then they are the ones who will reap the harvest.

Jesus himself taught this principle, which underlies his words in Luke 10:2,10-11. He insisted that it is foolish to spend time on rocky soil when there are fertile fields waiting to be sown and reaped. See also his saying in John 4:35, which again suggests the need to hasten into a field when it is "whitened", for if the church does not gather in the crop, another will.

AN INADEQUATE UNDERSTANDING

The common manifestations of such "revivals" [98] are reflections of an inadequate understanding of the gospel -

They display a failure to grasp the believer's righteous standing in Christ, which leads to a lack of spiritual authority. Without such a sense of irresistible spiritual authority the task of demolishing the ramparts of darkness and building the kingdom of God becomes impossible (cp. Je 1:9-10, 17-19). Sadly, few Christians have grasped the authority that belongs to them in Christ (Lu 10:19; Ph 4:13; Cl 1:10-13), or know how to use that authority to good effect.

---

98   That is, the kinds of intense emotional and physical reactions I have described above.

They display a failure to grasp the baptism in the Spirit, which leads to a lack of spiritual power.

Thus everywhere we see churches that lack the two things most necessary for fulfilling the evangel: authority and power. Churches often try to satisfy this lack by the substitute of "revival". But it will not do. Heaven expects us to seize all that belongs to us in Christ, and to fulfil the evangel with boldness. Why should God do for us what we can do for ourselves? A farmer most surely should pray for God's highest favour to rest upon his fields, his crops, his herds, but he can hardly expect the Lord to do the **work** of the farm! We must find a point of balance between the naturalism that banishes God altogether, and the supernaturalism that banishes man altogether. Whatever our own hand can achieve ought to be done by us - yet always asking God to "prosper the work of our hands", and always leaving room for him to do all that lies in heaven's prerogative -

> *"Look upon us kindly, O Lord our God, and make the work of our hands prosperous - Oh! do prosper the work of our hands!" (Ps 90:17; cp. also 1:3; 128:1-2).*

Further, a focus upon "revival" may actually be an excuse for throwing upon God the blame for our own lack of bold action. But when people are fully apprised of who they are in Christ, of where they stand in Christ, and of what they possess in Christ, and when they are walking in the fulness and power of Holy Spirit baptism, they do not feel any need of revival; quite the contrary, they see themselves as already enjoying continuous revival!

A SMALL EFFECT

Despite their spectacular nature, and the prominent place given to them in some evangelical church histories, "revivals" in general have had a small effect in comparison with what the larger church has achieved (even without Holy Spirit baptism) by patiently and methodically working at the unexciting task of planting multitudes of local congregations.

If you think about it, you will realise at once that across the centuries the overwhelming majority of Christians have been joined to the church outside of times of "revival"; very few of the present number of congregations and Christians world-wide were born in "revival". [99]

Or think about this. During the first centuries of Christianity, and despite the steady growth of the church, Roman society actually worsened, [100] until the empire finally collapsed. The church cannot by itself either change or save society. On the contrary, several of the emperors (including some of the noblest of Rome's rulers) persecuted the church; not because they were God-haters, but because they felt that Christianity was undermining the cohesion and strength of the empire! They saw the church as an enemy, not a friend.

Not even the late 4th century decree of Theodosius the Great, who made Christianity the only lawful religion in the empire, could stave off the utter ruin that barely a century later overwhelmed its western half. The eastern half, too, though it was thoroughly Christian, eventually collapsed under the battering of Islam. The Christian world was aghast, pondering the tragic mysteries of divine providence. Why did God allow another great religion to

---

99   Consider Australia again, which currently has some 10,000 Christian congregations (of all persuasions), with about 1.5 million people at church on any given Sunday; yet Australia has never had a nation-wide "revival". All those churches and all those people have come into being simply as a result of faithfully doing the work of the gospel year after year.

100   The value of the currency steadily decayed, ever more spectacular gladiatorial combats were staged with growing savagery, the formerly laissez-faire economy became increasingly feudal, the moral decline continued, slavery remained deeply entrenched, the conspicuous extravagance and self-indulgence of the wealthy created deeper chasms of bitter resentment, and ever-widening fractures appeared in the social and political structures of the empire.

spring up? Why did he permit the slaughter of multitudes of Christians? How could heaven stand idly by while Islam took possession of vast territories that had once been entirely Christian? [101] Since then all those lands have remained almost wholly Muslim. [102] Indeed, the church has never succeeded in taking back any territory that Islam has conquered.

Nonetheless, individual Christians must strive to be the "salt of the earth", and the eventual influence of the church is always toward social coherence, stability, justice, and godliness. In any case, whether or not the church is enjoying a rich harvest, there is never sufficient reason for Christians to fall into the fault taken up in the next heading -

AN UNHAPPY FATALISM

Perhaps the worst aspect of the "spiritual awakening" model is its tendency to induce a fatalistic and defeatist attitude. A focus upon "revival" seems to induce the corollary, that unless God does open the windows of heaven and pour down showers of blessing, the church will remain largely helpless and incapable of reaping a great harvest. Such an approach hardly reflects the brave faith, the bold endeavour, and the unshakable sense of triumph that moved the early church as it went out into the world to fulfil its missionary mandate.

---

101 North Africa, Egypt, Syria, Palestine, and substantial portions of Asia Minor and Eastern Europe.

102 Today, again, of course, Islam is by far the greatest threat confronting the church. Neither materialism, secularism, nor communism, were ever a serious peril; but a resurgent Islam, passionate, spiritually powerful, could well repeat history and carry multitudes of people away from the cross of Christ and put them under the crescent moon of Allah. Will that happen? I don't know. Partly the answer lies in how well the church does its work; partly the answer lies in world political changes and alliances; ultimately, the answer rests in the providence of God.

CONCLUSION

Two positive things must be said about the "spiritual awakening" model -

All Christians should desire a visitation of God, and should devote at least some prayer to that goal, in good hope of a gracious response from heaven. What could be more wonderful, more exciting, more glorious than to see the land shaken by the power of God? I am a preacher, how could I be other than delighted to see the preaching of the gospel prospering as never before?

Nonetheless, the scarcity of biblical support for such a model, and its often negative consequences, make it undesirable as our major definition of "revival". Some elements of the "spiritual awakening" idea we must keep; but we need to look for another model of revival, one that better reflects apostolic doctrine and practice.

Chapter Fourteen

SURE HARVEST

INTRODUCTION

Many of the things said above are also applicable to this "sure harvest model", so I will not repeat them. This model seems to me to reflect biblical principles more closely , yet still falls short of a truly apostolic focus.

DEFINITION

Two assumptions underlie the "sure harvest" model of revival -

The church has a missionary mandate, and it should not sit around praying and waiting for some arbitrary heavenly visitation, but should earnestly dedicate itself to fulfilling that mandate to the ends of the earth, and until the end of time.

The New Testament uses "harvest" analogies to describe the church and its mission; therefore it may be assumed that where the "sowers" of the gospel "seed" act in harmony with the laws of the harvest an abundant crop will be inevitable (Mt 13:3-9, 18-23; Mk 4:26-29; etc.)

DESCRIPTION

Adherents to this model depend upon careful planning, organisation, and presentation, and not upon any extraordinary supernatural intervention by God. Thus they do not focus upon crying out for a heavenly visitation, but rather for effective ways to present the gospel. Their aim is to compel a responsible assent by the sinner to the claims of Christ.

This model is best exemplified today in "the church growth movement". In the last century it was the major premise under-lying the ministry of the great revivalist Charles G. Finney.

ASSUMPTIONS

Once again, the foundation upon which the "sure harvest" model is built is the assumption that so long as the church works in harmony with the laws of spiritual harvest it can be sure of success. Just as God has promised that a farmer may be sure of his harvest if he does his work properly (Ge 8:20-22), so the laws of spiritual harvest are reckoned to be fully reliable. Spiritual law, it is said, is just as invariable and as trustworthy as the laws that govern natural harvests.

Proponents of this model believe that men and women can be, and will be, persuaded to accept Christ, if only the gospel is presented to them reasonably, and in a manner that utilises all the valid tools of persuasion. This does not mean that the influence of the Holy Spirit can be ignored; rather that God may be trusted to respond to a workman who is working well. Whether a man is toiling on a farm or in the field of souls, he may trust the spiritual principle -

> *"Put everything you do into the hands of God and your plans will be successful" (Pr 16:3).*

OBJECTIONS

Like the former model, this one plainly embraces much that is true; yet as a prime focus of Christian thinking on the subject of "revival" it seems deficient because -

It tends to ignore the fact that there are times of divine visitation, and that the church by diligent prayer sometimes can stimulate a supernatural intervention in the affairs of the community - or even of the nation. Although God cannot be compelled so to intervene, the church must ever be aware of the possibility of a divine visitation and must constantly pray for it. [103]

The "harvest" model ultimately reduces conversion to a human response to a set of propositions; salvation becomes a consequence of a cluster of planned stimuli. But note -

The presentation of the gospel may include both of those things, but it is also much, much more than a mere argument or a programmed stimulus. Sadly, people may hear the gospel in a perfect environment, and may even fully accept the biblical message, yet still fail to be born again. How can that be? For two reasons. First, because they love darkness more than light (Jn 3:19), and so refuse to believe. Second, because of the mysterious action of the Holy Spirit, who alone can impart new life. Thus, some people with defective knowledge may be given that life, while others with full knowledge may be denied it (cp. Jn 1:13; 3:8; 6:44; etc.) Indeed, if I am the one who persuades and "converts" someone, then he or she will probably soon be talked out of the faith again, and be gone. In the end, only those who are truly "born of the Spirit" can truly enter the church and remain there (cp. Jn 3:5-8; Jn 6:44).

CONCLUSION

No doubt we should work in the harvest field as wisely and effectively as we can, making use of every useful tool and every available resource. There is undoubtedly a general presumption in scripture that those who go out into the world "bearing precious seed" will come back again rejoicing in the harvest the Lord has given them (Ps 126:5,6). In that sense, the "sure harvest" model echoes biblical principles, and is closer than the "spiritual awakening model" to the general tenor of scripture.

---

103 Think about the several prophecies that have been given over the past decades, predicting a great revival in Australia and New Zealand. Time will tell how truly those oracles have spoken, but they certainly encourage hope of a powerful move of God across the land.

Yet this model also falls short of a true expression of the New Testament concept of "revival". So we must turn to a third model, and in this we shall find a completely satisfying focus for prayer and faith.

Chapter Fifteen

PENTECOSTAL EVANGELISM

INTRODUCTION

Both scripture and history show that there certainly are times of divine visitation, and there is no reason why God may not do again what he has done in the past. Consider these examples, out of many that are scattered across Christian history:

> ➢ the three astonishing years of Jesus' ministry

> ➢ the first few dramatic years in Jerusalem (Ac 2:43; 5:12-16)

> ➢ the world-changing Reformation in the 16th century

> ➢ the explosive Wesleyan revival in the 18th century

> ➢ and other such times of powerful spiritual awakening.

Yet we must acknowledge that, on the whole, those times have resulted from one or both of two major causes -

AN ESCHATALOGICAL INTERVENTION

That is, they were related in some way to a pre-ordained development in the kingdom of God. For example, the time of Jesus' ministry saw a divine visitation that was the presage of a new era in the unfolding of God's redemption plan for Israel and the nations (cp. Lu 19:41-44). In a similar way, the last days before the second coming of Christ have been promised a great outpouring of the Holy Spirit (Jl 2:28-31). The original Day of Pentecost, of course, led to the launching of the church.

When this eschatalogical element is present, the visitation will occur independently of any prayer or labour by the church, for the outpouring of the Spirit is part of the irresistible advance of God's programme for the ages.

A SOCIOLOGICAL ENVIRONMENT

By far the most common prerequisite for "revival" is a particular combination of social, political, and cultural conditions, allied with divine sovereignty. I think it could be shown, with very few exceptions, that "revivals" across the span of church history have occurred within a certain societal milieu, which has aroused a deep spiritual hunger in masses of people. That milieu may arise out of war, radical cultural change, economic depression, a reaction against materialism, anxieties caused by the collapse of familiar traditions and structures, and the like.

Two prime examples can be found in

(1) The 16th Century Reformation

In the time of Luther (1483-1546), the feudal structures of mediaeval Europe had collapsed, a new middle-class was rapidly emerging, cities and towns were gaining an importance and influence they had never before enjoyed, the old social fabric was shredded, and a new kind of society was emerging. Added to all this social disturbance was the cultural revolution that had begun a hundred years earlier, which we call the Renaissance. There was also the enormous impact of the recently invented printing press. The whole of Europe was undergoing a ferment of change at all levels and in many areas, all of which opened the way for the Reformers to preach their revolutionary gospel of grace and faith. So the Protestant churches were born, and the western world was changed for ever! A century or so earlier, or a century or so later, the same preachers would not have gained anywhere near the same response, nor made anything like the same impact.

(2) The 18th Century Wesleyan Revivals

Britain was then in the throes of the Industrial Revolution, and encumbered with a substantially lifeless Anglican Church. From being a largely rural culture, Britain was rapidly becoming industrialised and its empire was expanding world-wide. Old verities had collapsed; startling, radical, and disturbing changes were happening everywhere; people had lost their familiar moorings and were ready to hear a new message of hope and security. The Wesleys and Whitefield gave it to them. Vast crowds flocked to the meetings of the revivalists, and hundreds of new religious "societies" (which became Methodist churches) were established.

A similar pattern can be observed in almost all the revivals that have broken out over the centuries. That is, "revivals" seldom occur apart from a social, religious, cultural, political, or economic setting that creates an environment conducive to effective proclamation of the gospel. Without such an environment, the most fervent and persistent prayers will probably remain ineffective. [104]

The church should never lose hope of, nor stop praying for, such times. Yet their uncertainty, their normal dependence upon factors over which the church has no control, should preclude them from becoming a major focus of prayer. They have been useful in the past, perhaps even necessary, to replace the lack of a constant Pentecostal dynamic, but they should no longer be necessary now

---

104   For example, in 1517 Martin Luther nailed his famous "95 Theses" to the door of the castle church in Wittenberg, and sparked off the Reformation. Yet only 100 years earlier the Czech reformer John Huss, who preached the same ideas as Luther, had been burned at the stake. The "fulness of time" had not yet come; the setting was not yet right for the Protestant Reformation to grip the minds and hearts of the nations (cp. Ga 4:4).

that the full dimension of Pentecost has been restored to the church. [105]

Unfortunately, many Pentecostals and charismatics are still carrying with them the piety, the theology, the baggage, of their former churches, with the result they have not fully realised all that God has given them in the Holy Spirit. They are still controlled by the same presuppositions and motivations as those must be who are not baptised in the Spirit.

Nevertheless, the Pentecostal "revival" in our time has been the greatest in the history of the church - an unparalleled explosion of soul-winning and church-planting. More churches have been planted by the Pentecostals during the 20th century, and more people won to Christ, than has happened in any other century in church history.

Strangely, this astonishing harvest remains largely ignored by other evangelicals, because they often -

➢ reject pentecostal/charismatic theology, [106] and therefore treat as suspect whatever Pentecostals achieve, deeming it unworthy to stand alongside their own statistics; or they

➢ refuse to admit or face the growth statistics; preferring to emulate the proverbial ostrich and bury their heads in the sands of deliberate ignorance; or they

➢ reckon that the movement lacks the phenomena that many evangelicals suppose are the essential marks of a genuine revival; [107] or they

➢ renounce the movement for not changing society.

---

105 An exception, of course (as I have mentioned above), exists in the case of a "revival" that occurs within an eschatalogical context.

106 Particularly the linkage of glossolalia with Holy Spirit baptism, and the doctrine of healing in the atonement.

107 See above, under the "Spiritual Awakening Model".

The most serious objection is the last one. For example, I have several times heard something like this from evangelical friends (and enemies): "If you Pentecostals have so much power, how come you have so little impact on the larger community? Why are you not changing the world, like Luther did at the time of the Reformation?"

But that is an invalid complaint, for our situation is more like that of the first century than the sixteenth. Consider this -

1. At the time of the Reformation the church was deeply woven into the social fabric - as the church went, so went the cities and the nation. When a prince or monarch converted to the new Protestant faith, he could (and did) oblige the entire population to convert also. Furthermore, the whole of Europe (as described above) was ripe for revival when the Reformers began their revolutionary ministry. By contrast,

2. At the time of the Early Church three centuries were to pass before any significant change was effected in the patterns and lifestyle of the Roman Empire. Indeed, the worst persecution the church ever had to face occurred in the early 4th century under the emperor Diocletian, when Christians still numbered probably less than half the population (of some 200 million). Only after the accession of Constantine the Great (in 310) did the church finally achieve legal status. Then at last it had opportunity to shape significantly Roman culture and the civil, social, religious, and legal foundations of the empire.

Likewise, if Jesus tarries, it may well require another two or three centuries before the impact of the Pentecostal revival of this century can begin to show any considerable influence upon society. [108]

---

108 For example consider this. After nearly 100 years of witness in Australia, Pentecostals in 1994 numbered barely 1.2% of the population (some 200,000 people in about 2000 churches). Even if we increased tenfold, to 12% of the population and 20,000 churches, we would still represent only

Despite the above, let us recognise that changing society is incidental to the primary purpose of the gospel, which is rather to "call out a people for his name" (Ac 15:14). Our aim is not the creation of Christian nations, but rather the building of the Christian church; the kingdom of God does not consist of national governments but of a holy people, whether they be few or many.

DEFINITION

While acknowledging that there is much truth in both of the former models, we look for a dynamic new approach to revival. It is a model that goes right back to the New Testament, and it can be defined as: evangelism in the power of the Holy Spirit. This model has two corollaries -

Dependence upon the confirmatory effect of the charismata

> see Mk 16:15-20; Lu 24:49-50; Ac 2:1-4; 4:29-31; 6:8; 14:3; Ro 15:18-19; Ga 3:5; 1 Th 1:5; He 2:4; etc.

spiritual authority based on the revelation of the believer's status

> that is, a revelation of the position every Christian has as the righteousness of God in Christ, enthroned with Christ in the heavenlies, possessing all the spiritual authority necessary to overcome Satan and to fulfil the calling of God (Ep 1:16-23; Cl 1:9-14).

If either one of those dimensions is missing, then the model will fail.

Some people, for example, understand the concept of spiritual authority, but lacking Holy Spirit baptism are unable to make effective use of it; while others, who have received Holy Spirit

---

a minority group; yet our church attendance would then exceed that of any other denomination. We have, I should think, at least another 100 years of work ahead of us before we can hope to be anywhere near that happy result!

baptism are equally ineffective, because they have not grasped the authority needed to utilise the power of the Spirit.

DESCRIPTION

The Acts of the Apostles provides the best demonstration of this "Pentecostal evangelism model", and surely represents the example that we should be striving to follow.

What is that example?

Surely one of bold and successful mission, by Spirit-filled men and women who know who they are in Christ, who utilise the full potential of the Holy Spirit, and through whom the charismata (1 Co 12:4-11) are abundantly expressed.

ASSUMPTIONS

PRAYER

The first assumption is prayer, which must undergird and be threaded through every aspect of the life and work of the church. However, the dominant focus of that prayer should not be a slippery "revival" that keeps on hiding itself; nor should it be the hope of finding some magic "key" that will enable the church to "break through". If such a key were available, why didn't Jesus know about it (cp. Lu 10:13-16); why didn't Paul, or any other apostle, find it; and why is there no instruction about it in the New Testament?

The main focus of prayer in the "Pentecostal revival model" is not that of crying out for some hoped for visitation, but rather that of the New Testament, which had four important thrusts -

1. Toward being filled with the Spirit

    ➢ but note that this infilling is a promise to be appropriated by faith, not a random act of divine caprice; cp. Ac 2:38-39; 4:29-31; Ep 5:18-19.

2. Toward gaining a revelation of the Word

   ➢ especially of our position and spiritual authority in Christ; see Ep 1:16-19; Cl 1:9-14; etc.

3. Toward releasing the charismata

   ➢ for they alone can empower the church to do and be as Jesus himself would if he were here in person.

4. Toward creating a peaceful environment

   ➢ in obedience to the mandate given in 1 Timothy 2:1-4.

Thus equipped, the church becomes truly the "body of Christ", taking the place of Christ in each local community, doing the works of Christ among the people (Jn 14:12-13), enabling the Lord to "confirm the preaching of the word with signs and wonders" (Mk 16:19-20).

Note the substantive difference between praying for an uncertain outpouring of the Holy Spirit, which is thought not yet to have come (and which may not come at all), and praying for a powerful release of what one already possesses. The first has no scriptural warrant; the other fills almost every page of the New Testament!

ACTION

The New Testament model is not passive, but active. It is not one of helpless Christians waiting anxiously for a divine visitation, but of Spirit-filled Christians moving out audaciously in full partnership with God. It is not a scene of ill-equipped people desperately longing for "revival", but of richly-armed warriors going out to overcome the world by the power of the Holy Spirit.

The assumption in the New Testament is that if the church can seize the fulness of the Holy Spirit, display the charismata, and grasp the revelation of its righteousness and authority in Christ, then all else will follow as a natural consequence.

Note again Paul's prayer in Ephesians 1:15-23. Here is an apostle praying for a local church; what will occupy his mind? Does he plead for "revival", for a great visitation of God upon Ephesus, for a plentiful harvest of souls, for the demonic forces in Ephesus to be overthrown, or for any of the other things that continually (and mostly vainly) occupy the prayers of multitudes of Christians?

No, he focuses upon only one thing: that they might gain a revelation of who they were, and what God had given them, in Christ! [109]

COMMANDS

As a consequence of the above, the basic commands in the New Testament may be summarised as

- ➢ believe the truth (2 Th 2:13)
- ➢ be filled with the Spirit (Ep 5:18)
- ➢ stir up the gift (2 Ti 1:6; 1 Ti 4:14)
- ➢ utilise the gifts (Ro 12:60)
- ➢ do the work (1 Co 15:58).

That work is primarily to plant churches, for there is no better tool of evangelism than a local church. No one has yet found a better way to win souls or to change the world than to plant first one church, then a score of churches, then hundreds, then thousands.

Note that even a person who is unable to grow any more than a small congregation in one place, can yet multiply his or her success by planting several small churches, or by training others to go out and plant churches.

---

109 Note: he had no need to ask God to give the Ephesians either Holy Spirit baptism, or the charismata, for they were already in enjoyment of both those blessings (Ac 19:6; Ep 1:13).

There is enough in those five commands to fill by themselves a large book! Suffice it here to note that they do not include praying for some elusive "revival" - a concept that is altogether lacking from the thinking of the apostles!

CONCLUSION

In the "Pentecostal evangelism model" there are plainly elements of both the former models; that is

    1. There is a sense of God promoting a spiritual awakening through the preaching of the Word in the power of the Spirit, and of the Word being supernaturally confirmed. But there is no sense of having to wait until God deigns to pour out his Spirit in response to the constant pleading of his people. The Day of Pentecost has happened; the Spirit is already given; now we need only receive the gift of the Spirit and then begin to live and work in the power of the Spirit. Those who keep on pleading for "another Pentecost" are actually telling God that the first one was faulty, which I for one do not believe!

    2. There is also a sense of working according to a plan, with a general expectation of a harvest, but no sense that the harvest is inevitable.

The New Testament paradigm is clear: in any given time or place the church may experience either prosperity or persecution; it may reap a vast harvest, or no harvest; it may be received or rejected (cp. Mk 6:4-6a; Lu 10:10-12; 2 Ti 1:15; and note the wide diversity of results that Paul experienced in different towns and cities - from outright rejection, to modest response, to astonishing success). Our task is not to produce a given result, but to be faithful in fulfilling the call of God. In the end, the best definition of revival lies in that one word: faithfulness

BIBLIOGRAPHY

Christian Ministry, The; William H. Willimon Art. (Nov/Dec) 1992.

Among God's Giants; J. I. Packer; Kingsway Publications Ltd. Eastbourne, Sussex; 1991.

Ballads Of A Bohemian, Robert Service; Pub. T. Fisher Unwin, London, 1921.

Bible and Sword; Barbara W. Tuchman; Pub. Ballantine Books; New York, 1956.

Book of Margery Kempe, The; tr. by B. A. Windeatt; Penguin Books, 1988.

Books and Parchments, The; F. F. Bruce; Revised and Updated; Pub. Fleming H. Revell Co.; Old Tappan, New Jersey, 1950.

Building the Church God Wants; Ken Chant; Vision Pubishing, Australia 1996.

Bursting the Wineskins; Michael Cassidy; Pub. Harold Shaw; Wheaton, Illinois, 1983.

Canterbury Tales; Geoffrey Chaucer (1345-1400), tr. Nevill Coghill; Penguin Classics; 1977.

Chronicles of Captain Blood, The; Rafael Sabatini, 1931.

Chronicles of the Crusades; ed. Elizabeth Hallam; Weidenfeld and Nicolson; London, 1989.

Discovery; Ken & Alison Chant; Vision Publishing, Australia, 1991.

Equipped To Serve; Ken Chant; Vision Publishing, Australia, 1995.

Essentials of Evangelism; Tom Malone; Bob Jones University; Sword of the Lord Publishers; Murfreesboro, Tennessee, 1958.

Eusebius' Ecclesiastical History; Pub. Baker Book House; Grand Rapids, Michigan, 1955.

Fortunes of Captain Blood, The; Rafael Sabatini; Pan Books; London, 1963.

Four Tragedies and Octavia; Seneca; tr. by E. F. Watling; Penguin Classics, 1970.

Georgics, The; Book One; Publius Vergilius Maro (Virgil) (70-19 B.C.); tr. K.R. Mackenzie; Folio Society, London, 1969.

Grand Tour, The: (1592-1796); ed. by Roger Hudson; Folio Society; London, 1993.

Gulliver's Travels; Jonathan Swift (1667-1745); Oxford University Press; New York, 1977.

Heart of Fire; Barry Chant; Luke Publications; Fullerton, South Australia, 1971.

Histories, The; Volume One; *Henry IV*; William Shakespeare; Heritage Press; Norwalk, CT.

History of Christianity, A; Volumes I & II; Kenneth Scott Latourette; Revised & Edited; Pub. Harper and Row; New York, 1975.

Jerome (circa 342-420); *Letters.*

Lives of the Artists in Three Volumes; Georgio Vasari; tr. by George Bull; Folio Society; London, 1993.

Meditations of Marcus Aurelius, The; tr. by Maxwell Staniforth; Penguin Books; 1986.

Mountain Movers; Ken Chant; Vision Publishing.

Pentecostal Movement, The; Donald Gee, Revised and Enlarged; Elim Pub. Co. Ltd. Clapham Cr. London, 1949.

Personality Type and Religious Leadership, Roy M. Oswald and Otto Kroeger; Alban Institute; New York, 1988.

Pillow Book of Sei Shonagon, The; tr. by Ivan Morris; Penguin Classics; 1967.

Poems of Robert Browning, The; Selected & Edited. by C. Day Lewis; The Heritage Press; Norwalk, CT, 1971.

Problem of Wineskins, The; Howard A. Snyder; Inter Varsity Press; Downer's Grove; Illinois, 1977.

Prophet, The; Kahlil Gibran; Alfred A. Knopf Publishers; New York, 1968.

Religio Medici, *The Faith of a Physician*; Sir Thomas Browne (1605-82) J. M. Dent & Sons Ltd. London, 1956.

Sartor Resartus; *Heroes and Hero Worship;* Thomas Carlyle; Published by J. M. Dent & Sons Ltd. London (1795-1881) Reprinted 1913.

Sirach; Old Testament Apocrypha.

Team Method of Church Planting, The; James H. Feeney; Abbott Loop Christian Center; Anchorage, Alaska, 1988.

Team Ministry; Dick Iverson; Bible Temple Publications; Portland, Oregon; 1984.

Under the Greenward Tree; Thomas Hardy; 1872.

Valley of Fear, The; Sir Arthur Conan Doyle (1859-1930).

We Can Take the Land; Ron Simpkins; Potters Press; Prescott, Arizona, 1984.

Week on the Concord and Merrimack Rivers, A; Henry David Thoreau (1817-62) Heritage Press; Norwalk, CT, 1975.

World Evangelisation Now by Healing and Miracles; Gordon Lindsay; Pub. Gordon Lindsay; 1951.

Wycliffe Biographical Dictionary of the Church, The; Elgin Moyer (1890), Revised and enlarged; Earle E. Cairns; Moody Press; Chicago, 1910.